SECRET RICHMOND UPON THAMES

Andy Bull

AMBERLEY

This book is dedicated to the memory of three great Richmond historians: Albert Barkas, Richmond's librarian from 1891–1921, who gathered thirty volumes of notes about the town's past; H. M. Cundle, who shaped those notes into a book, Bygone Richmond, which was published in 1925; and John Cloake.

First published 2020

Amberley Publishing
The Hill, Stroud
Gloucestershire, GL5 4EP

www.amberley-books.com

Copyright © Andy Bull, 2020

The right of Andy Bull to be identified as the Author of this work has been asserted in accordance with the Copyrights, Designs and Patents Act 1988.

ISBN 978 1 4456 9882 3 (print)
ISBN 978 1 4456 9883 0 (ebook)

British Library Cataloguing in Publication Data.
A catalogue record for this book is available from the British Library.

Origination by Amberley Publishing.
Printed in Great Britain.

Contents

Preface

Richmond-upon-Thames is a very royal town. Yet, despite the fact that it was home to a string of monarchs over 700 years, and it is the site of four former royal palaces, almost all trace of this royal heritage vanished long ago. Also generally forgotten is that the borough was home to a seventeenth-century royal tapestry works where sumptuous wall hangings were created for St James's Palace, Kensington Palace, Windsor Castle and Holyrood Palace. We shall explore the remarkable stories, and reveal the secrets, of these long-lost places.

Richmond is also home to rock 'n' roll royalty, yet, while it is well-known that Mick Jagger of the Rolling Stones lived on Richmond Hill, and Pete Townshend of The Who still does, it is far less well-known that, alongside them, fellow Stone Ronnie Wood, Ronnie Lane of The Faces and – during particularly difficult periods in each of their lives – Eric Clapton, and Syd Barrett of Pink Floyd have all lived on the Hill.

Richmond is the final resting place of three of the greatest explorers, one hugely famous in Canada, the other in Australia, but all three virtually forgotten in England.

There is also the tale of Charles Darwin and the plot to destroy Kew Gardens, and the story of how the town came to be home to two remarkable organisations dedicated to the long-term welfare of those whose lives have been shattered by war.

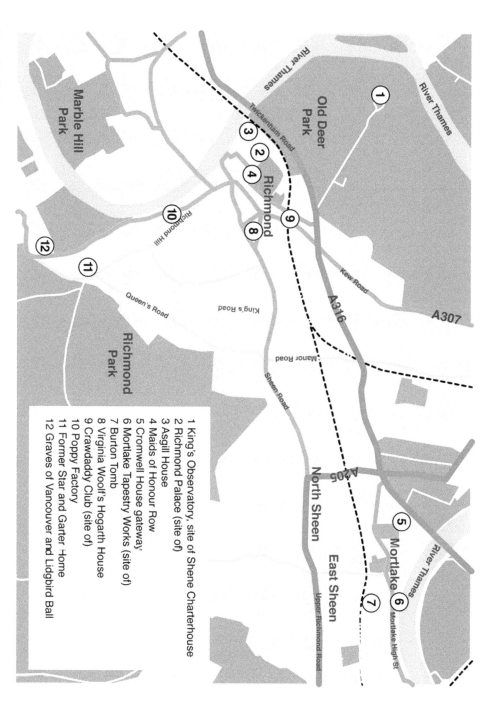

Map: Emily Duong.

1 King's Observatory, site of Shene Charterhouse
2 Richmond Palace (site of)
3 Asgill House
4 Maids of Honour Row
5 Cromwell House gateway'
6 Mortlake Tapestry Works (site of)
7 Burton Tomb
8 Virginia Woolf's Hogarth House
9 Crawdaddy Club (site of)
10 Poppy Factory
11 Former Star and Garter Home
12 Graves of Vancouver and Lidgbird Ball

1. The Palace on Richmond Green

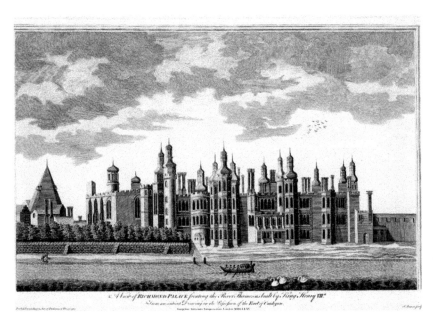

Richmond
Palace in
Henry VII's
time.

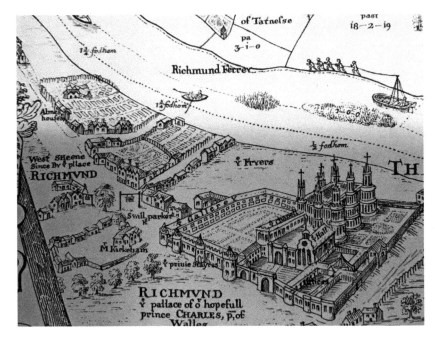

Richmond
Palace on
Moses
Glover's
map of 1635.

Between Richmond Green and the River Thames stood a royal palace which, as it evolved over five centuries, was lived in by monarchs including Edward III, Henry VII, Henry VIII, Elizabeth I, Charles I and II. Henry I began the royal connection in 1126, when just a manor house stood on the site. The last king to use it – as a royal nursery – was James II, in 1688.

Today, only the gatehouse and a short terrace remain of what was Shene Palace (under various spellings) until renamed Richmond Palace by Henry VII when he rebuilt it in 1501. However, by gathering fragments of evidence – the few sketches, plans and maps that exist, and what little archaeological work has been done on the site – it is possible to uncover the secrets of the palace, and build a vivid picture of what it looked like, how it functioned, and to establish the backdrop to the remarkable events that occurred here.

DID YOU KNOW?

Shakespeare's plays were regularly performed by him and his company before Elizabeth I at Richmond Palace. On one occasion, according to H. M. Cundall in *Bygone Richmond*, the queen flirtatiously dropped her glove before Shakespeare, who was playing the part of a king, as she crossed the stage to her seat. Remaining in character, the Bard picked up the glove, improvised the line 'And though now bent on his high embassy, yet stoop we to take up our cousin's glove', left the stage and presented it to the queen, who was apparently delighted.

The Gatehouse on the Green

One invaluable key to Richmond Palace in its final, grandest manifestation is Moses Glover's Map of the Hundred of Isleworth, made in 1635, soon before it was torn down during the Commonwealth. Stand on Richmond Green and look south towards the Thames and you face the gatehouse, now incorporated into Palace Gate House, as depicted on Glover's map. This was the principal access to the palace on the landward side. Henry VII's coat of arms is displayed above the entrance.

Moses's map shows a crenelated guard wall, with a series of turrets, running to left and right where there are now a series of eighteenth-century houses.

Not all stories handed down about the palace and its occupants are true. Among the false tales is that Elizabeth I died in the room above the gateway. She didn't. The supposed death chamber was in fact just a room built to accommodate porters who attended the main gate.

Elizabeth, who was imprisoned here for a time during the reign of her half-sister Mary I, lived and died (in 1603) in the royal chambers, or Privy Lodgings, at the other end of the palace. Despite her earlier experience, this became Elizabeth's favourite residence. She particularly liked it in winter, when it was the warmest of all her palaces.

The Gatehouse from Richmond Green.

Henry VII's crest on the gatehouse.

The Wardrobe, in Old Palace Yard.

Old Palace Yard

Walk through into Old Palace Yard and, then as now, you are in a large courtyard. This was called New Court in 1445, and later Great Court. The terrace to the left is The Wardrobe, where clothing and soft furnishings were stored when not in use. This building is mainly Tudor, and once had an arcade beneath it, where carts could be unloaded. The arches were blocked up, and large sash windows added, during extensive alterations in the late seventeenth and early eighteenth centuries. Behind The Wardrobe was a tennis court.

To the right of Old Palace Yard, where Stables Cottages have stood since the 1950s, were stables, workshops and the clerk of works' office.

Burghley House, closely modelled on the Privy Lodgings at Richmond Palace. (Anthony Masi under Creative Commons 2.0)

Trumpeters' House

Directly ahead, Trumpeters' House replaces the three-storey stone Middle Gate building. A sketch by the Flemish topographical artist Antony Wyngaerde, dated 1562, shows it with an archway and oriel window above and, on the left of two thin turrets, one of the trumpeter figures which gave the present house its name.

The gateway to the palace went right through the front door and out of the back of the present building. Beyond this gateway was a second courtyard, named Middle Court, or Fountain Court. To the right, as shown in Wyngaerde's sketch, was the Great Hall and, to the left, the chapel. Beyond the courtyard can be seen the heart of the palace: the many-turreted Privy Lodgings.

By the seventeenth century, when the palace was in ruins, Middle Gate housed the gardener who looked after the gardens that had by then replaced the chapel, Fountain Court and the Privy Lodgings. A diplomat called Richard Hill leased the land and built Trumpeters' House in the early eighteenth century, incorporating some of the Middle Gate building, and mounting the two stone figures of trumpeters which had adorned the old gate on the new house. Trumpeters' House was converted into four flats and a small house, Trumpeters' Lodge, in the 1950s.

Trumpeters' House replaces the Middle Gate building.

Wyngaerde's 1562 sketch looking over Middle Gate into Fountain Court, with the Privy Lodgings beyond.

Fountain Court, the Great Hall and Chapel

The Great Hall was enormous, 45 feet tall and 200 feet long, with a great domed, louvred central lantern to let out smoke from the fire that would have burned in the centre of the floor. The chapel was also of stone, hung with cloth of gold, and the altar set with relics, jewels and rich plate. On 5 January 1511 Henry VIII's son with Catherine of Aragon, who had been born at the palace at New Year, was baptised Henry in the chapel. He lived only until 22 February.

Catherine of Aragon with Henry VIII. (Wellcome Collection)

The servants' entrance to the palace ran from Old Palace Lane.

To reach the Privy Lodgings, you would have left Middle Court via a bridge over a moat, which enclosed the heart of the palace on three sides, the fourth being guarded by the Thames itself.

Old Palace Lane

To the right of Trumpeters' House, on the south side of the entrance from Old Palace Lane, is Trumpeters' Inn, a row of houses built in 1956 on the site of the kitchens, and other domestic offices.

The kitchens were extensive, and included a privy kitchen for preparing the royal family's food, a livery kitchen for the rest of the household, meat and fish larders, a poultry house, a pastry kitchen and brewery. There was also a coal store and woodyard, and a large communal lavatory, draining into the moat, which would have been cleared by the rising and falling tides. Eschewing such a facility, Elizabeth I made the palace one of the first buildings in history to be equipped with a flushing lavatory, invented by her godson, Sir John Harington.

Old Palace Lane, which leads to the Thames, was used from the fourteenth century as the tradesmen's and servants' entrance to the palace. Goods were transported here by barge, offloaded onto a jetty by crane, and then brought up the lane – which was originally called Crane Piece. Remnants of a later jetty are still there, and posts – two of which have been dated to 1585 – are visible at very low tides.

In 1972, when new houses were built at No. 27–30 Old Palace Lane, in the area where the lane meets the side entrance, evidence was discovered of the western arm of the moat leading down to the Thames.

Edward III's Palace

From opposite The White Swan pub down to the river is the site of the manor house of Shene, used by Henry I from 1126. From 1363–68, Edward III converted it into the first royal palace. Information is too sketchy for a detailed plan to be drawn, but there would have been an 'over court' towards the green and a 'down court' towards the river, the two parts divided by the moat. It was to the west, or downriver, of the later palace.

In 1383, when Richard II married Anne of Bohemia, they chose Shene as their principal royal residence. They were in their teens and turned their arranged marriage into a love match. Shene was their favourite house, and Richard had a pavilion built on an island in the Thames as a romantic retreat. However, when in 1394 Anne died of the plague, the distraught king cursed the palace and ordered that it be completely destroyed, and the site was abandoned.

This area was later planted as the Great Orchard. Records show that, in 1649, it contained 223 fruit trees, with a further 170 around the walls.

Asgill House

Asgill House, on the site of Edward III's palace.

Today, Asgill House stands on the former orchard. It was built by Sir Charles Asgill, Lord Mayor of London, from 1757–62. By the middle of the last century the house, which had been insensitively altered with the addition of two side wings, had fallen derelict and the Crown Estate, which still owns the palace area, considered demolishing it. However, Asgill House was restored, the later additions removed, and it is now Grade I listed.

A New Palace Is Built

In 1414, Henry V built a new palace, in a project described as 'the kynges grete work', moving it just upriver, to what is now the lawn leading down from Trumpeters' House to the Thames. In 1545, Henry VI did more work, all of which was undone forty-eight hours before his successor, Henry VII, was to celebrate Christmas Day here in 1497. A great fire broke out which destroyed most of the palace. Undeterred, Henry VII set about building a sumptuous replacement which, in 1501, he renamed Richmount (Richmond) after the earldom he held in North Yorkshire.

In 1998, Channel Four's *Time Team* excavated, and identified the exact location of the Privy Lodgings – the grand centrepiece of Henry VII's creation. The square building was three storeys tall, with a tower at each corner and four or five along each side. Most of the towers were topped with pepper-pot domes set within battlements. In the north-east corner was a four-storey tower which was described as 'a chief ornament unto the whole fabric', with a substantial room on each floor and a staircase of 120 steps. Perhaps surprisingly, the area where the royal apartments stood has never been built on.

Henry VII, who rebuilt the palace after the great fire of 1497.

Holinshed's
depiction of the fire.

The king and queen's apartments overlooked the Privy Orchard and Privy Gardens on the eastern, upriver, side. Francis Bacon, who wrote a biography of Henry VII, said 'the king had at his death, mostly in secret places under his own key and keeping at Richmond, £1.8m, a huge sum of money'. That sum equates to £2.4bn today, according to the Bank of England's inflation calculator. Henry died at the palace in 1509.

In 1530, Henry VIII forced Cardinal Wolsey to swap Hampton Court Place for Richmond Palace and then, in 1540, gave Richmond to his fourth wife, Anne of Cleves, in their divorce settlement.

Friars' Ground
The next section upriver, beyond the site of the Privy Orchard and Privy Gardens, is the area between Friars Lane and Water Lane. While the new palace was being built for Henry VII, he needed somewhere to stay, and had a timber, lath and plaster royal manor house at Byfleet dismantled and moved here. This temporary palace was substantial, with royal apartments for king and queen, a chapel, and all necessary ancillary buildings to service the royal family and house a substantial retinue.

When, by 1499, it was no longer needed, he gave it to an order of Franciscans – Grey Friars. The friary was suppressed in 1543, during the Reformation, and the land sold off for secular use. In the eighteenth century, several grand houses were built on parts of the Privy Orchard and Privy Gardens, and a number have fascinating stories connected to them.

Cholmondeley House, and the Girl with Two Fathers
Cholmondeley House was built in the corner of the old Friars' Ground, beside the river, by the Earl of Cholmondeley, who leased a large part of the former orchard and gardens. He already leased The Wardrobe, and obtained, according to John Cloake in his *Richmond*

Palace: Its History and Its Plan, a 45-foot-wide strip of land running from behind The Wardrobe down to the river. In around 1738 he built a library which encroached on the riverside walk, and was granted the whole of Friars' Ground in return for maintaining a pedestrian right of way – Cholmondeley Walk – alongside the river. In around 1748 he completed Cholmondeley House, and Friars' Lane was diverted to dog-leg around the new building.

In 1780 Cholmondeley House was bought by William Douglas, 4th Duke of Queensbury and one of the most prominent characters in George III's court. John Cloake comments,

> Old Q [as he was known] was one of Richmond's outstanding characters: a dandy and a wit, with a passion for gambling, horse racing, music and the fair sex, he entertained lavishly and gave generously to charity ... Here the notorious duke lived for some years entertaining in a munificent manner members of the royal family and many celebrities of the time.

In another house, facing the river, lived Queensbury's friend George Selwyn, a prominent politician. Upon their deaths both men gave substantial bequests to a young woman called Maria Fagnani, known as Mie Mie – Queensbury leaving her his house, and Selwyn leaving her a large sum of money. Why? Because of a curious agreement between them regarding Maria.

The story is an intriguing one. Maria's mother was the Marchesa Costanza Fagnani, a married Italian noblewoman who met and began an affair with Henry Herbert, 10th

Cholmondeley House.

The site of the Privy Gardens.

A surviving stretch of Tudor wall beside Queensbury House.

Earl of Pembroke. Eloping with him to London, she was introduced to Queensbury, with whom she also began an affair. In 1771, Queensbury sent a letter to Selwyn to tell him that the previous evening the Marchesa had given birth to Maria, and that he was the father.

For reasons that are unclear, he persuaded Selwyn to take custody of the child and raise her as his own, which lead to assumptions that it was actually Selwyn who was her father. Later, when the Marchesa had returned to her husband in Italy, she asked Queensbury to intervene and have Selwyn return Maria to her, which he did. However, soon regretting his decision, Selwyn begged the Marchesa to return the girl to him. She did so, in return for his making Maria his heir.

In 1798, Maria married the Earl of Yarmouth, heir of the Marquess of Hertford. William Makepeace Thackery parodied Hertford as the Marquess of Steyne in *Vanity Fair*. Yarmouth had great influence with the Prince Regent, who made him vice-chamberlain of his household. Maria's charms were such that, when King George III was insane, he announced that he was going to take her as his mistress. Maria seems to have had little interest in the house she had been left, and it fell into decay.

Further up Friars' Lane is a block of flats called Queensbury House, which in 1933 replaced a mansion of the same name built here in 1830. Just beyond the block is a stretch of Tudor wall that once divided the Privy Orchard from the Privy Garden.

Old Palace Place and the Former Friary

To the east at the top of Friars' Lane is Old Palace Place in which, on the site of the friary, stand two houses, Old Palace Place itself and Old Friars. Both bear traces of the friary. The

Old Friars, former home of Sir Richard Attenborough.

Maids of Honour Row.

south-west corner of Old Palace Place, build around 1700, is Tudor and includes a vaulted basement with fireplace and bread ovens, a beamed, galleried landing, and a bedroom with powder room, all dating from 1580. During the First World War the house was used as a Red Cross hospital, and Lord (Kenneth) Clark, of *Civilisation* fame, lived here in 1930–32.

Old Friars, thought to have been built in 1687, the date marked on a rainwater pipe, was home to the actor and director Richard Attenborough and his wife Sheila Sim for fifty-three years until 2012. The extension, Beaver Lodge, was built in around 1740 as a concert room and called the Great Room on the Green.

Maids of Honour Row

Although the Hanoverian monarchs did not live at Richmond Palace, preferring other locations in the area, they did continue a connection with it. While the future George II lived with his wife Caroline at Richmond Lodge in Old Deer Park, in 1724–25 he built a terrace of four houses on the edge of the former Privy Garden and facing the green, initially to house Caroline's ladies-in-waiting, or Maids of Honour as they were then called.

No. 4 became the home of John James Heidegger, master of the revels to George I and George II.

2. Richmond's Rock 'n' Roll Royalty

Richmond Hill has been a fashionable place to live since the eighteenth century. The unparalleled views from the hill over the Thames as it meanders through Ham and Petersham have, in the past, attracted the likes of the artist Joshua Reynolds and the playwright Richard Sheridan to live in its grand houses.

In the latter half of the twentieth century the hill attracted hugely successful artists from a different field: rock 'n' roll. Mick Jagger, Eric Clapton, Pete Townshend, Ronnie Wood and Keith Richards have all lived here. Just down the hill, in Petersham, lived Prince Rupert Loewenstein, the man credited with making the Stones the most financially successful band in the world.

In the 1960s Richmond was also the birthplace of a musical revolution, in which an emerging generation of brilliant young musicians took gritty R&B, fused it with electric rock and roll and began to define a sound that would sweep the world. Richmond's Crawdaddy Club, together with the Ealing Blues Club and Eelpiland on Eel Pie Island, Twickenham, were the cauldrons in which that revolution was forged. Richmond Hill was also home to a menswear shop that catered for the sartorial tastes of this new movement.

The famous view from Richmond Hill.

Richmond Hill has been fashionable since the eighteenth century.

The Crawdaddy Club

It was only because Giorgio Gomelsky knew the landlord of the Station Hotel, and heard that the jazz sessions held in a hall at the back of his Kew Road pub were a flop, that Richmond became a crucible in the formation of British rhythm and blues, pop and rock.

And it was only because a group called the Dave Hunt Band were stuck in a snowdrift during the worst winter for generations that a young, unknown group called the Rolling Stones were allowed on stage. They were not a big draw. Only three people turned up and Gomelsky, a twenty-nine-year-old assistant film editor with a love of music and a flair for promotion, had to trawl through the hotel bars to get any sort of a crowd.

This performance, on Sunday 24 February 1963, was the Stones' first since Charlie Watts and Bill Wyman had joined Brian Jones, Mick Jagger and Keith Richards to complete the line-up. Gomelsky spotted their potential, and the Stones were given a two-gig-a-week residency. Word spread fast, and within three weeks their gigs were packed, the crowds boosted by Gomelsky's offer of a free ticket to any punter who brought two friends along.

Gomelsky, an emigre from Soviet Georgia who had fled Stalinist terror with his parents in 1938, played a large part in managing and promoting the band. He persuaded the Stones, who were short of enough material to fill two forty-five-minute sets, to finale with a twenty-minute version of *Crawdad* by Bo Diddley. In these early weeks the club had no name, but when a journalist asked Gomelsky what he should call it, he thought of that song, and came up spontaneously with The Crawdaddy.

On 14 April the Beatles came to see the Stones, and afterwards went back with them to their flat in Edith Grove, Chelsea. Another who came to a Crawdaddy gig was Andrew

The former
Crawdaddy Club.

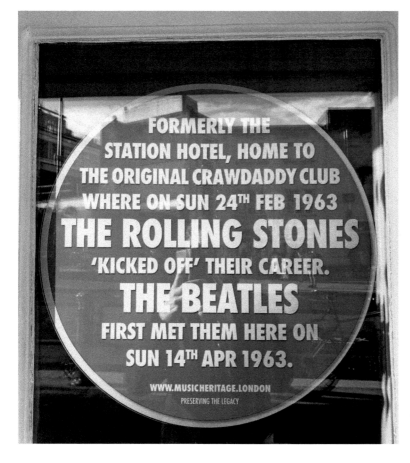

Musical heritage
at the former
Station Hotel.

Rolling Stones Mick Jagger and Keith Richards. (Larry Rogers Under Creative Commons 2.0)

Loog Oldham, who became their manager. The first ever review of the Rolling Stones appeared in the *Record Mirror* in May 1963:

> At the Station Hotel, Kew Road, the hip kids throw themselves about to the new 'jungle music'... and the combo they writhe and twist to is called the Rolling Stones ... Three months ago only fifty people turned up to see the group. Now ... over 500 fans crowd the hall ... unlike the other R&B groups worthy of the name, the Rolling Stones have a definite visual appeal.

However, the Station Hotel's owners, Ind Coope, were horrified at what they considered the degenerate behaviour portrayed in such articles and banned the club. Gomelsky was forced to move the Crawdaddy across the A316 to a larger venue beneath the grandstand at Richmond Athletic Ground.

In June '63, the Stones had their first hit single, a cover of Chuck Berry's *Come On*, and had outgrown even this larger venue. Their residency was taken over by The Yardbirds, featuring Jeff Beck and Eric Clapton. Led Zeppelin, Elton John, Rod Stewart and Long John Baldry would also play the Crawdaddy.

Giorgio Gomelsky went on to champion many other promising musicians. He managed The Yardbirds and founded a record label, Marmalade. He released early recordings by Jeff Beck and Jimmy Page, Rod Stewart, Graham Bond, Soft Machine; and Graham Gouldman, Kevin Godley and Lol Creme, who went on to have a string of huge hits as 10cc. In 1978 he moved to America, where he championed a range of avant-garde bands, and became a pioneer of music video. He died in 2016, aged eighty-one.

DID YOU KNOW?
When the Railway Tavern in Kew Road was known as The South-Western, a young Eric Clapton played here in The Roosters, along with Tom McGuinness, later of Manfred Mann and The Blues Band.

Rock Royalty on Richmond Hill

There was just one problem when, in 1971, Ronnie Wood fell in love with The Wick, an elegant, twenty-room, Grade I listed Georgian house with spectacular views from its perch on the edge of Richmond Hill: the actor Sir John Mills wanted £100,000 for it, plus £40,000 for the cottage at the bottom of the garden, and Ronnie could raise only £28,000 from the sale of his existing house.

The Wick.

Keith Richards and Ronnie Wood. (Raph PH under Creative Commons 2.0)

Wick Cottage.

Wood, who was then in The Faces, the band fronted by Rod Stewart, managed to scrape together just enough for the main house, but could not stretch to buying the cottage as well. It looked like what he has described as 'the most beautiful house in the world' would slip through his fingers, until he had a brainwave, and managed to persuade fellow band member Ronnie Lane to buy the cottage.

House and cottage became party central, with a string of musicians popping round to jam with the two Ronnies – Paul McCartney, David Bowie and Greg Allman among them. In 1973 Eric Clapton came to stay. At the time, Clapton was seeking to overcome his heroin addiction and stage a comeback. Pete Townshend of The Who stepped in to help, and rehearsed with him and Ronnie for two weeks at The Wick. Both appeared alongside Eric at two gigs held on 13 January at The Rainbow in Finsbury Park. The concerts were recorded for a live album, *Eric Clapton's Rainbow Concert*, released that September.

A year or two later, Keith Richards, lead guitarist in the Rolling Stones, came over to The Wick one evening and ended up staying four months. Eventually he moved into the cottage, which Ronnie Lane had left to go travelling in a gypsy caravan. Ronnie Wood wrote the following in his autobiography, *Ronnie*:

> We never thought about asking Keith to leave because we were having too much fun producing great songs with great mixtures of different musicians, and those months just flew by ... those early days with Keith opened the door to the Stones. But they also gave me great confidence musically. We were making fabulous music in a buzzing environment and The Wick had a revolving door populated with the world's top musicians.

I Know It's Only Rock 'n' Roll was written here, during a jam between Ronnie Wood, Keith Richards, David Bowie, and Mick Jagger. In 1975, Ronnie joined the Stones.

Keith's presence brought a drug raid. Ronnie writes, 'They'd been staking out the cottage ... from a hotel room at the top of Richmond Hill for a month. One night they decided to sweep [but] Keith hadn't been there for two weeks.' They found only Ronnie's wife Krissy at home, in bed together with her girlfriend, and a trace of cocaine. No charges were brought.

The Wick, which stands at the top of Nightingale Lane and was built in 1775 on the site of the Bull's Head Tavern, had been bought by Sir John Mills, star of *Ice Cold in Alex*, *In Which We Serve* and *Ryan's Daughter* in 1956. The sound of the wind around the house reputedly inspired his wife, Mary Hayley Bell, to write *Whistle Down the Wind* – later filmed staring the couple's daughter Hayley Mills – in a gypsy caravan in the garden.

In 1996 Pete Townshend bought The Wick. Ironically, the sound of the wind whistling through the gaps in the house's original windows caused him huge problems. In 2010 it was reported that the high-pitched tone so aggravated the hearing problem he had developed after years of performing at ear-shattering decibels that it was 'driving him mad'. He had to have the windows replaced.

A few years before Townshend moved to Richmond Hill, Mick Jagger had bought Downe House, just across the road and a little down the hill from The Wick. He lived there with his wife, the model Jerry Hall, until they separated in 1999. Jerry Hall remained in Downe House while Jagger moved into a flat next door. In the eighteenth century, Downe House was owned by Richard Sheridan, the playwright, satirist and owner of the Theatre Royal, Drury Lane.

Another musician to have lived on Richmond Hill was Syd Barrett, original frontman of Pink Floyd and writer of early hits *Arnold Layne* and *See Emily Play*. He was brought to live in a second-floor flat here in 1967–68 with Floyd's keyboardist Richard Wright while the band were struggling to get the increasingly paranoid Barrett off LSD and on to stage. The flat was owned by the family of Pink Floyd's co-manager Andrew King. While Syd was there, the band realised they could not save Syd, and decided to recruit Dave Gilmour to replace him.

Richard Wright told Mark Wilkerson, author of *Pigs Might Fly: The Inside Story of Pink Floyd*, that he was faced with the unwelcome task of lying to his flatmate when he went off to perform without him: 'I had to say things like "Syd, I'm going out to buy a pack of cigarettes" and then come back the next day.' Syd went on to have an erratic solo career and died in 2006.

Pete Townshend bought The Wick from Ronnie Wood (Kubacheck under Creative Commons 2.0)

Downe House, former home of Richard Sheridan and Mick Jagger.

DID YOU KNOW?
Sir John Mills bought The Wick twice. His daughter, the actress Hayley Mills, wrote, 'My parents sold the Wick when I was 12, but my mother missed it terribly. It was where she had been happiest – when her children were little ... A few years later, my parents happened to have dinner with the people who had bought The Wick. When Daddy told them that Mummy had never got over the loss of the house, they said, "Well, we're selling it. Perhaps you'd like to buy it back." So they did. They returned there when I was 16 and kept it for another seven years.'

Mick Jagger and Prince Rupert, the Man Who Made the Rolling Stones Rich

Apart from the fact that his house – Petersham Lodge, at River Lane in Petersham – was just down the hill from Mick Jagger's, it would be hard to imagine how these two men could have anything in common. Prince Rupert Loewenstein was a pin-striped, Bartok-loving German aristocrat who, as president of the British association of the Sovereign Military Order of Malta, was one of the most senior Roman Catholics in Britain; Jagger was the extrovert, outrageous frontman in the greatest rock and roll band in the world, a man who had once confessed to *Sympathy for the Devil*.

In fact, Prince Rupert was a key member of the Rolling Stones' entourage for forty years, and the mastermind behind the band's financial success.

When Loewenstein, who could trace his royal lineage back to 1474, was introduced to Jagger by a mutual friend in 1968, he had never heard of the band. However, when the two got talking they found they had a fundamental interest in common: money. Jagger had become increasingly angry that the vast majority of the money the band made went to their then manager, Allen Klein. Loewenstein, who when they met was managing director of Leopold Joseph, a small London merchant bank, got them out of onerous contracts, had them move to France to avoid punitive UK tax rates of up to 98 per cent, and showed them how to make vast sums from world tours.

Until they parted ways in 2007, Loewenstein was, Mick once said, 'a combination of bank manager, psychiatrist and nanny'.

Loewenstein's wife, Josephine, told *Tatler*, 'We became great friends and travelled with the band on many tours. But it was hard work for Rupert at the beginning. There were a lot of substances, which was difficult for him because he didn't do any of that kind of thing. And so he was really working at night, because in the day they were asleep. It was very trying.'

Loewenstein, who died in 2014, wrote in his autobiography, *A Prince Among Stones*, that he and Jagger

Petersham Lodge, former home of Prince Rupert Loewenstein.

... clicked on a personal level. I certainly felt that [he] was a sensible, honest person. And I was equally certain that I represented a chance for him to find a way out of a difficult situation. I was intrigued. So far as the Stones' music was concerned, however, I was not in tune with them, far from it. Rock and pop music was not something in which I was interested ... After the first two or three business meetings with Mick, I realised there was something exceptional in his make-up, that his personality was able to convert his trade as itinerant performer into something far more intriguing.

DID YOU KNOW?
There is a shrine to Marc Bolan, whose glam rock band T Rex were one of the biggest stars of the mid-1970s, at the site where he died on Barnes Common. Bolan, who lived nearby at No. 142 Upper Richmond Road West in East Sheen, died in 1977 when his purple Mini, driven by his girlfriend Gloria Jones, left the road, crashed into a steel fence and came to rest against a sycamore tree. In 1997 a memorial stone and bronze bust were unveiled by his son, Rolan Bolan, at the spot, near Gipsy Lane on Queen's Ride.

The Marc Bolan Shrine on Barnes Common. (Britmax under Creative Commons 2.0)

The Ivy Shop

For the Crawdaddy's musicians and their fans, image was vital. However, the clothes they wanted, in which they could achieve the apparently effortless American Ivy League cool of the post-war years, were hard to get hold of in the UK. Until, that was, the summer of 1964, when an East End tailor called John Simons opened the Ivy Shop at No. 10 Hill Rise, Richmond Hill, offering just that style. It was a Mod look: soft-shouldered, single-breasted suit jackets; slim-fit trousers; Oxford shirts; and penny loafers.

Simons had expected his shop to appeal to Richmond's young, style-conscious businessmen. He told *The Guardian,*

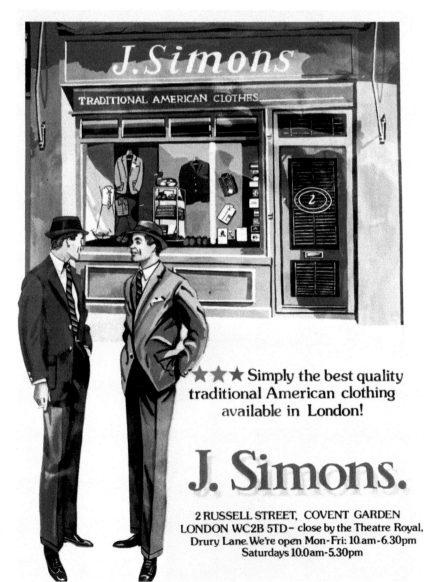

★★★ Simply the best quality traditional American clothing available in London!

J. Simons.

2 RUSSELL STREET, COVENT GARDEN
LONDON WC2B 5TD – close by the Theatre Royal,
Drury Lane. We're open Mon-Fri: 10.am-6.30pm
Saturdays 10.0am-5.30pm

John Simon, owner of Richmond's Ivy shop, opened a second store in Covent Garden in 1981.

It was people who wanted to dress like Jack Lemmon in *The Apartment* that we really wanted to attract, but that never happened. All the Jack the lads came instead ... it was a look which middle and working-class kids wanted and were prepared to pay for. The Ivy look became a massive hit and the place to get it was the Ivy Shop in Richmond ... It was an egalitarian tradition for a society that didn't really have a lot of history in that way. It was like Savile Row for everyone.

It was Simons who spotted that golfing jackets he had newly acquired from the British clothes manufacturer Baracuta – with elasticated waist and cuffs and a tartan lining – were like those worn by Ryan O'Neal, who played a character called Rodney Harrington in the TV soap *Peyton Place*. He put them in the window of the Ivy Shop with a note pointing out the similarity. The name stuck and Harrington jackets became a Mod essential.

In 1981, Simons opened a second shop, J. Simons, in Russell Street, Covent Garden, moving to Marylebone in 2011. Richmond's Ivy Shop closed in 1995.

3. Royal Parks

Richmond Park is among the most famous and well-known places in London, but there are many secrets to be revealed about this royal playground, as there are about the Old Deer Park, which has a much longer, more obscure connection with royalty.

Old Deer Park and the Lost Village of West Sheen

For centuries, Old Deer Park ran right up to the north side of Richmond Green and Richmond Palace, but is now separated from it by the railway line, the A316, and a band of housing. One park feature no longer evident was a great Carthusian monastery which bordered the Thames. Moses Glover's Map of the Hundred of Isleworth, made in 1635, shows the Charterhouse of Jesus of Bethlehem of Shene, which was founded in 1414 by Henry V. No sign of it remains above ground today, but the foundations of the priory church lie beneath the fairway and fourteenth hole on the Royal Mid-Surrey Golf Course.

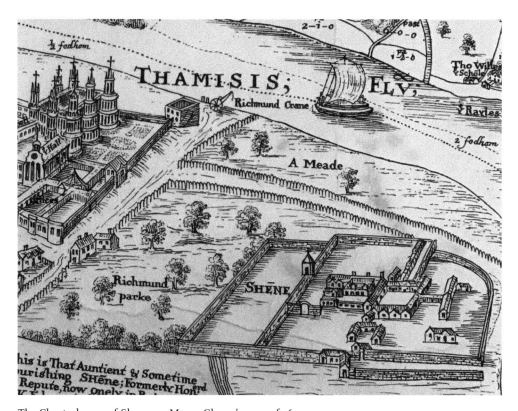

The Charterhouse of Shene on Moses Glover's map of 1635.

Old Deer Park. (Amanda Slater under Creative Commons 2.0)

The King's Observatory, Old Deer Park. (Simon Tompsett under Creative Commons 2.0)

It was an impressive place: with a river frontage of 3,000 feet, a great hall 132 feet long and cloisters measuring 600 feet, around which were cells for thirty monks. It was one of a pair of religious houses built by Henry V, the other being a convent of the Bridgettine Order established across the river where Syon House now stands. He did so in an attempt to expiate the crimes of his father Henry IV, who deposed his cousin Richard II. Richard starved to death in prison.

Shakespeare refers to the two religious houses in *Henry V*. In the king's speech before the Battle of Agincourt, there is a reference to 'Two chantries where the sad and solemn priests still sing for Richard's soul'.

The Charterhouse was surrendered to Henry VIII, restored, then finally dissolved in 1558, after which it became a palace known as Sheen Place, and changed hands many times. H. M. Cundall, in *Bygone Richmond*, recounts that houses were erected around it, to serve this rich manor, and the village of West Sheen was formed. In 1604, James I created New Park for Richmond Palace, covering all the former Charterhouse land apart from that occupied by the buildings. In 1637, when Charles I created Richmond Park, it became known as Little Park or Old Park, and then Old Deer Park.

A hunting lodge, Richmond Lodge, was built the following year, as a home for the keeper of the park, to the north-west of the monastery buildings. Over the decades the house was gradually extended and improved by subsequent owners. In 1704 it was rebuilt by the Duke of Ormonde, who held the crown lease. Ormonde, however, was stripped of the land when he became involved in a plot to prevent George I's accession to the throne, and in 1715 it became the country residence of the Prince of Wales. When the prince took the throne as George II, in 1727, he and his wife Caroline made Richmond Lodge their country residence. They converted a large portion of the park into pleasure gardens.

DID YOU KNOW?
While George II and his wife Caroline lived at Richmond Lodge, two of their servants were bitten by a rabid dog. The pair were rushed to Gravesend and dipped into the waters of the Thames Estuary – it being believed at the time that salt water could guard against rabies. As an intended mark of their loyalty to the royal household, residents of West Sheen shot all dogs within a mile of the lodge.

The Royal Observatory, and a Palace That Never Was

Richmond Lodge passed to George III in 1760 and became his principal retreat, where the royal family would stay each June to October. There were plans to replace the lodge with an entirely new building, which would take the name Richmond Palace. Through the centuries the monastery buildings had been disused, and by the time of the Commonwealth (1649–60) they were derelict. When George III came to plan his palace, he hired Capability Brown to create one of his fashionable swept landscapes, in which sunken ha-has were used to invisibly delineate the borders of his creation. At the same time the remaining monastery gateway was pulled down, all surviving traces of the chapel, great hall, cloister and other buildings removed, and the hamlet of West Sheen obliterated to make way for the new palace.

There was also to be an observatory attached to it. George was fascinated by science, and observing the heavens had become hugely fashionable among those wealthy enough to own sufficiently powerful telescopes. George was keen that the observatory be completed before the transit of Venus across the sun, which was to occur on 3 June 1769. This was to be a hugely significant event, enabling astronomers to calculate with greater accuracy the size of the solar system, and the distance between the earth and sun. A few years later, the observatory was the scene of an even greater scientific advance. It was used to successfully test a marine chronometer, designed by John Harrison, that enabled mariners to calculate their longitude at sea.

The Palladian observatory, surmounted by a cupola to hold the telescope designed by Sir William Chambers, was the only part of the palace to be built. It passed out of royal hands in 1840 and, renamed Kew Observatory, was administered by first the British Association for the Advancement of Science, then the Royal Society, and finally the Meteorological Office. In the mid-nineteenth century it was an important centre for research into the sun and its influences on the earth, geomagnetism and meteorology.

George III:
fascinated by
science and
the heavens.
(Wellcome
Collection)

HIS MOST GRACIOUS MAJESTY KING GEORGE THE THIRD.

A special telescope was developed here, called a photoheliograph, which could take photographs of the sun, and Kew played a vital part in discovering the connection between solar flares and disturbances in the earth's magnetic field. It was the Met Office's main observatory, at which experiments were made in using automatic instruments to record the weather, and essential, systematic records were kept of key meteorological phenomena including temperature, atmospheric pressure and humidity.

The Met Office moved out in 1980 and the building was converted into offices, reverting to its original name. It became a private house in 2014, and occasional tours are available.

The Three Royal Palaces of Kew Gardens

Until the eighteenth century, Old Deer Park and Kew Gardens had been divided solely by a path, Love Lane, that led from Richmond Green to the horse ferry from Kew to Brentford. Kew End Road, which runs from the A316 along the east side of Old Deer Park, is the surviving stump of that route, but its line is still followed within Kew Gardens by Holly Walk. In 1785, an act of parliament allowed George III to unite park and gardens by closing Love Lane, ensuring royal privacy. The two were separated again in 1841, when the Royal Botanic Gardens, a public body now sponsored by the Department for the Environment, took over the running of Kew Gardens.

Today, the name Kew Palace relates to the red-brick, Dutch-gabled building close to the main entrance, but there have been two other royal palaces in the area: the White House, and the Crenelated Palace. It was Caroline, wife of George II, who first used accommodation at Kew, in 1728, when she found Richmond Lodge too small to host all her family. She occupied Kew Palace, which had been built in 1631 by a wealthy French Huguenot merchant. However, this wasn't big enough for Prince Frederick, George II's heir, and he used a larger house next door, Kew House. It was remodelled by William Kent and renamed the White House. Frederick was to die at Kew before he could inherit the throne, catching pneumonia while gardening.

George III used Kew Palace as a home for his fifteen children. Each baby would stay with its mother, Charlotte, at Richmond Lodge for the first year, then move to Kew and

The surviving Kew Palace. (Ethan Doyle White under Creative Commons 2.0)

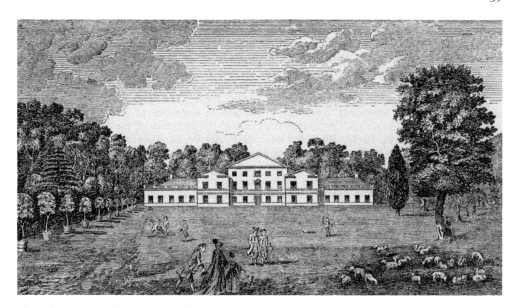

The White House: the second royal palace at Kew, demolished in 1802.

The Castellated Palace, the third royal residence at Kew, was never completed.

be placed in the care of a governess. In 1772 king and queen also moved to Kew, living rather like country gentry, in contrast to the life they led at other, grander palaces. After George III's madness became apparent, in 1788, he was confined to Kew during attacks, but allowed to live at Windsor Castle once they had passed. He was given a couple of ground-floor rooms at the White House, while his doctors and equerries filled a wing. The rooms above George's apartment were kept empty so that his ravings could not be overheard.

Despite his illness, George III planned a new residence at Kew. Building began on a Gothic Castellated Palace on the riverside, and the White House was demolished, in 1802, in anticipation of the Castellated Palace becoming the prime royal residence. However, George died before it was completed. Building stopped, and it was later demolished and replaced, in 1828, during the reign of George IV, by a house that was also subsequently pulled down. A sundial, placed just west of the present Orangery, marks the spot. It bears the initials of William III, and was moved here from Kensington Palace by William IV.

Richmond Park

It was Charles I who created Richmond Park, in 1637, calling it Richmond New Parke to distinguish it from the existing park, which became known as Old Park. Charles loved hunting, and found Old Park too small, so decided to create an enclosure of 2,400 acres between the two palaces of Hampton Court and Richmond, and to stock it with red and fallow deer. The move was unpopular, involving the creation of an 11-mile-long enclosing wall that took in formerly common lands at Richmond, Petersham, Ham, Kingston, Roehampton and Mortlake, plus farms and smallholdings.

H. M. Cundall, in *Bygone Richmond*, says,

Charles I, creator of Richmond Park.
(Wellcome Collection)

A deer in the former royal hunting ground of Richmond Park. (Drow Male under Creative Commons 2.0)

Many refused to give up their land for the king and when the wall – which still stands – began to go up a fierce clamour arose. It was too near London not to be the common discourse there.

Much pressure was used to prevent Charles from proceeding with his design, but neither the disapprobation of the people, nor the appeals of those in high authority, had any effect ... The king's action in this respect was one of the primary causes of his unpopularity.

As a concession, ladder stiles were placed so that the walls could be scaled, and the roads remained open to the public.

DID YOU KNOW?
George II kept large flocks of turkeys in Richmond Park, which were hunted by dogs and forced to take refuge in the trees where they were fired on by the king and other huntsmen.

Pembroke Lodge

Maps from 1754 and 1771, where it is marked as Molecatcher's, reveal the trade of the original inhabitants of Pembroke Lodge. The molecatcher was moved out after Elizabeth, Dowager Duchess of Pembroke – Queen Charlotte's former Lady of the Bedchamber – fell in love with what was then a cottage, and persuaded George III to let her live there. The house was enlarged, and she stayed here until her death in 1831. Subsequent monarchs continued to use the lodge as a grace and favour residence. In 1847 Victoria gave it to her

Pembroke Lodge, once called The Molecatchers. (Patche99z under Creative Commons 2.0)

then prime minister, Lord John Russell. On summer Sunday afternoons he held soirees attended by leading politicians and literary figures. Today it is a popular wedding venue.

King Henry's Mound

The popular story behind the naming of the mound that stands in Pembroke Lodge Gardens is that Henry VIII stood at this point while awaiting a signal from the Tower of London that his wife Anne Boleyn had been executed. However, the story is implausible, because at the time of Anne's beheading, midday on 19 May 1566, Henry was at Wolf Hall in Wiltshire, over 50 miles away. Also, H. M. Cundall reports, accounts differ as to what sort of a signal Henry might have been looking out for. Some chroniclers say it was the sound of a gun being fired, others the flash of a gunshot, some that a signal would be given using a black flag, others that a rocket would be fired. As the tower is 11 miles from Richmond Park, it is unlikely that any of these signals could be made out from the mound.

Old documents show the mound has had other names at different times. In the year the park was enclosed, a plan names it as 'The King's Standinge', which could refer to the park's creator Charles I, and indicate the vantage point he used when surveying the work being undertaken. One further suggestion is that Charles I stood here during hunts, firing at deer that were driven past on the flat land below.

On a 1745 map it is named Oliver's Mount. This may refer to the time, in November 1647, when Cromwell amassed a large Parliamentarian army at Ham, and may have stood here to review his troops.

White Lodge

White Lodge, now home to the Royal Ballet School, was another grace and favour residence. It was built by George II as an occasional residence, first called Stone Lodge. He had created the mile-long avenue, Queen's Walk, leading from the lodge, and it became his wife Caroline's favourite walk. According to a map of 1745, there was a road, called the Queen's Private Road, leading to the park's Queen's – or Bog – Gate from Richmond Lodge in the Old Deer Park, and crossing present-day Kew Road, Upper Richmond Road

White Lodge, home to the Royal Ballet School. (BarnyS1 under Creative Commons 2.0)

and Sheen Common on its route. While the royal couple were at White Lodge, Richmond inhabitants were allowed to walk in the gardens of Richmond Lodge.

George II passed the lodge to his daughter, Princess Amelia, when he appointed her Ranger of the Park. Amelia caused uproar when she severely restricted public access. A pass was required, and very few were issued. Two lawsuits were brought by Richmond residents in an attempt to get the order overturned. The first, concerning access for carriages, she won. The second, involving a Richmond brewer called John Lewis, in 1758, and concerning access on foot, she lost. As a result, ladder stiles and gates were added to Sheen Gate and Ham Gate. In celebration, a great crowd came from a wide area and poured into the park.

Lewis became a local celebrity. His portrait was painted by Joshua Reynolds, and hangs in the reference library at the Old Town Hall. Lewis is buried on the southern side of Richmond churchyard.

George III gave White Lodge to his deputy park ranger, Viscount Sidmouth, who was visited by Nelson on his journey to Portsmouth and his ship, HMS *Victory*, on the eve of the Battle of Trafalgar. H. M. Cundall relates that Nelson dipped his finger into his wine and sketched out his battle plan on the tablecloth. Queen Victoria would later live here for a short time.

Sheen Lodge

Sheen Lodge, which stood beside Sheen Gate, was another elegant house with humble beginnings. It was originally a small thatched cottage used by keepers, and named The Dog Kennel on early plans. It was used by huntsmen, and had kennels for their hounds.

It was enlarged by George III as another grace and favour apartment. Queen Victoria gave it to Sir Richard Owen, a scientist who had taught her children natural history, and who would become the first director of the Natural History Museum. Owen was a man who brought his work home with him. His wife wrote in her diary that he once arrived with the remains of a hippopotamus that had died at London Zoo, and dissected it in the house. In 1842 Owen coined a name for the extinct creatures he had been studying when he suggested they should be called 'Dinosauria', after the Latin for 'terrible lizards'.

Sheen Lodge was the scene for a royal proposal of marriage when, in 1893, Queen Victoria's grandson Prince George – the future George V – proposed to Princess Mary of Teck, who was living with her mother at the White Lodge. This was Mary's second royal proposal. Just over a year before, she had become engaged to George's brother, Prince Albert. Sadly, Albert had died of pneumonia a month into the engagement.

Close to the lodge once stood an ancient ash tree known as the Shrew Ash, about which there have been various superstitions over the centuries. Under one, from the seventeenth century, sick children were pushed through a split in the trunk in the hope of a cure. The tree was also thought to be able to cure ailments in cattle. A hole would be bored into the trunk, a shrew placed inside and the hole sealed with clay. It was believed that, if a branch were taken from the tree and cattle hit with it, any ailment would be cured.

Sheen Lodge suffered bomb damage in February 1944, and was destroyed by fire that October.

DID YOU KNOW?
Buccleuch House, which once stood in Buccleuch Gardens, was home to a slave who became hugely famous as a composer, playwright and connoisseur of art and music. Ignatius Sancho, who was born on a slave ship, became butler to the Duke of Montagu and, although entirely self-taught, established himself as a fashionable and respected figure in eighteenth-century society, corresponding with eminent men including David Garrick and Lawrence Sterne, and having his portrait painted by Thomas Gainsborough in 1768.

Sir Richard Owen once dissected a hippopotamus at Sheen Lodge. (Elliott and Fry under Creative Commons 2.0)

4. Richmond and the Arts

Virginia Woolf

Virginia Woolf is most readily associated with Bloomsbury, through her membership of the Bloomsbury Set, but it was in Richmond that she found her voice as a writer and, with her husband Leonard, established the Hogarth Press, which became a hugely influential publishing house and brought out works by T. S. Eliot, one of the most famous poets of the twentieth century, and Katherine Mansfield, one of the finest writers of short stories.

Virginia and Leonard Woolf came to Richmond in 1914, staying first in rented rooms at No. 17 The Green, then moving the following year to Hogarth House at No. 34 Paradise Road, which they saw on a walk and fell in love with.

They had come to Richmond for Virginia's mental health. In 1913, aged thirty-two, she had suffered a nervous breakdown, during which she took an overdose of veronal, a barbiturate then used as a sleeping pill. Doctors wanted to have her committed to an asylum, but agreed that, as an alternative, Leonard could take her away from central London to a peaceful place where he and nurses could care for her.

Richmond did the trick, and Virginia became much happier. She said of the town that it was 'the first of the suburbs by a long way, because it is not an offshoot of London, any more than Oxford or Marlborough is' and that Hogarth House, which she would live in until 1924, was 'a perfect house, if ever there was one ... far the nicest house in England'. For a time it seemed they might not secure the lease, and Virginia recorded in her diary, 'We walked after lunch in the Park, and came home by way of Hogarth, and tried to say that we shan't be much disappointed if we don't get it.'

At the same time as moving to Hogarth House they decided to buy a printing press, initially so they could take up printing and book binding as a hobby that would relieve the stress that writing, and submitting her manuscripts to publishers, caused Virginia.

She famously said that a writer needed 'a room of one's own' in which to practise their craft, yet she generally wrote the first draft of novels including *Night and Day*, *Jacob's Room*, and *Mrs Dalloway* sitting in an armchair before the living room fire in Hogarth House. She placed a piece of board, onto which she had glued an ink pot, across her knees and wrote, as Leonard said in his memoirs, 'with concentrated passion'.

Virginia recorded in her diary, 'So I made up *Jacob's Room* looking at the fire at Hogarth House ... There's no doubt in my mind that I have found out how to begin (at 40) to say something in my own voice.' From 1922, Virginia published all her own novels.

She credited their Richmond home as being behind the enterprise which gave them financial security, writing, 'Nowhere else could we have started the Hogarth Press, whose very awkward beginning had rise in this very room, on this very green carpet.'

A myth has developed, however, that Virginia disliked Richmond. The source of this misconception can be traced to the 2002 film *The Hours*, in which Nicole Kidman, playing Woolf, has the line, 'If it is a choice between Richmond and death, I choose death.'

Right: Virginia Woolf. (George Charles Beresford)

Below: Hogarth House, No. 34 Paradise Road, where Virginia and Leonard Woolf founded the Hogarth Press.

In 2018 a plan to erect a life-size bronze of Virginia Woolf in Richmond was approved. Depicting her sitting on a bench, it will be placed on Riverside.

George Eliot

Mary Ann Evans moved to East Sheen in April 1855 to live with George Henry Lewes, a married man with three children, in a cottage at No. 7 Clarence Row, since demolished, but which stood on the corner of Sheen Lane.

George Eliot.

The move from north London was prompted because, while many Victorian men had mistresses, the couple scandalised society by living openly as man and wife. In fact, Lewes had an open marriage with Agnes Jervis, and she had a relationship with, and children by, another man. The move came as a great relief. Marian wrote to a friend, 'We are panting to be in the country and resume our old habits of undisturbed companionship and work.'

That September they moved again, to a second-floor room at No. 8 Parkshot, Richmond, where Marian called herself Mrs Lewes so as not to shock their landlady. A. Leonard Summers, in *The Homes of George Eliot*, describes it as

> ... an unpretentious-looking Georgian house, ivy-clad, but suitable on account of its quiet and seclusion, though in close proximity to the railway station ... at the back was a long narrow garden, enclosed by a high, ivy-covered wall.

While in Richmond, Mary Ann adopted the pen name George Eliot – in order, she said, to have her work taken seriously – and wrote her first novel, *Scenes of Clerical Life*. *Adam Bede*, also written in Richmond, earned the then substantial sum of £1,705 (around £215,000 today). She went on to write *Mill on the Floss* and *Middlemarch,* and establish a reputation as one of the greatest nineteenth-century novelists.

George Lewes had submitted Mary Ann's first manuscript to the Edinburgh publisher John Blackwood, saying it was from a shy male friend. According to the *Oxford Dictionary of National Biography,*

Blackwood actually began corresponding, via Lewes, with [his author]. He knew he was dealing with a potentially great writer, telling his mysterious correspondent in January 1857 that he had recently confided to Thackeray that he had 'lighted upon a new author who is uncommonly like a first class passenger'. Mary Ann replied to this praise on 4 February 1857, signing herself for the first time George Eliot.

For two years, authorship was attributed to a man from the Midlands called Joseph Liggins, although Charles Dickens guessed when he read the first book that it was by a woman. It was only when Blackwood visited the Leweses at Richmond that he discovered his star writer was female.

On the manuscript of *Adam Bede* held at the British Library, Marian wrote this dedication: 'To my dear husband, George Henry Lewes, I give this M.S. of a work which would never have been written but for the happiness which his love has conferred on my life.'

Eliot loved walking in Richmond Park, and the view from Richmond Hill. She wrote,

On our way to the Park the view from Richmond Hill had a delicate blue mist over it, that seemed to hang like a veil before the sober brownish-yellow of the distant elms ... As we came home the sun was setting on a fog-bank and we saw him sink into that purple ocean – the orange and gold passing into green above the fog-bank, the gold and orange reflected in the river in more sombre tints.

The couple left Richmond for Wandsworth in 1859. The house at No. 8 Parkshot was demolished in 1905 and replaced with an office building. This was replaced in 1975 by a new magistrates' court, and that building was converted into offices in 2017.

Edmund Kean

The hugely celebrated Shakespearean actor Edmund Kean spent his final years in Richmond, where in 1831 he formed a company and took on the lease of the King's Theatre, later the Theatre Royal. The theatre, which had opened as the New Theatre in 1765, stood on the south-west side of the Green, at the top of Old Palace Lane, and was a scaled-down copy of the Theatre Royal in Drury Lane. Kean lived in two rooms in the house next door.

This was very much the twilight of the great actor's career alcoholism meant he could not learn new parts, but he survived by reprising his Shylock in Shakespeare's *The Merchant of Venice* and other mould-breaking performances. Shylock was a role he had first performed at Drury Lane in 1814, in a naturalistic style that was a revelation to audiences used to declamatory, histrionic acting, and it had sealed his fame. He performed at Richmond several times between 1818 and 1820, when at the height of his powers.

In 1830 Kean, learning that the lease at Richmond was available, saw an opportunity to realise a long-held dream of managing his own theatre and company. This was not, however, a gentlemanly retirement: Kean continued to perform at other theatres in London and the provinces. At Richmond, he struggled to attract sufficient audiences during his tenure but still managed to turn a profit, and was hugely popular in the town.

Mr KEAN as Richard

Left: Edmund Kean as Richard III.
(Metropolitan Museum of Art)

Below: Kean's plaque in Richmond's church,
now moved from above his grave to the wall.

Beneath this stone lies
EDMUND KEAN
Actor · DIED 1833
'The sun's bright child'

In 1832 Kean carried on a local tradition and offered a wherry – a light cargo or passenger boat – as a prize to be rowed for by local boatmen. The boat was hauled on stage at the theatre for the presentation ceremony.

During his Richmond years, Kean's health deteriorated rapidly. The actress Helena Faucit Martin, in *On Some of Shakespeare's Female Characters*, gave a vivid description of him in his final years:

> a small pale man with a fur cap, and wrapped in a fur cloak. He looked to me as if come from the grave. A stray lock of very dark hair crossed his forehead, under which shone eyes which looked dark, and yet as bright as lamps. So large were they, so piercing, so absorbing, I could see no other feature.

Kean was unable to continue his performance of *Richard III* at Richmond on 12 March 1833, and had to leave the stage. Despite that, he was back on the boards three days later. His final performance was as *Othello* at Covent Garden on 25 March where, sadly, he collapsed during the second act. Kean was taken to a nearby inn, where he was put to bed. Five days later he returned to his rooms at Richmond, where he died on 15 May, aged forty-five.

According to his actor son Charles, who was on stage with him at that final performance, two women claimed to be Edmund Kean's mother, a Mrs Carey and a Mrs Tideswell. Mrs Carey nursed him during his fatal illness and died a few days after him. Unable to decide which of these 'mothers' to believe, Kean provided for both of them in their old age.

His funeral in Richmond was almost a state occasion. A huge cortege made its way from the Green to the parish church of St Mary Magdalen, where Kean was buried in a vault beneath the south aisle. Charles had a memorial erected to his father outside the church and close to his grave, but it was moved in 1866 when the church's south-west porch was built, and the exact location of the vault was lost. Today a slate memorial plaque is to be found within the church.

After Edmund Kean's death the theatre declined, and the last performance was held in 1857. It was demolished in 1884.

DID YOU KNOW?
After the Theatre Royal, managed by Edmund Kean in later life, closed in 1884 there was no permanent theatre in Richmond. Sensing a business opportunity, Francois Chrysostome, who owned the Castle Assembly Rooms in Whittaker Avenue, hired Frank Matcham, renowned architect of the London Palladium and The Coliseum, to design a new theatre with a highly ornamented façade of red brick and terracotta on Little Green. It opened in 1899, as the Theatre Royal and Opera House. It went through several name changes, including to the Hippodrome in 1908, before settling on Richmond Theatre.

Mrs Dorothea Jordan

An earlier performer at the theatre was Mrs Dorothea Jordan, who also happened to be the mistress of the Duke of Clarence, later William IV, from 1791–1811. They lived together for a time at Petersham Lodge, River Lane, Petersham, a house that would later be owned, as we saw in chapter 2, by Prince Rupert Loewenstein, financial advisor to the Rolling Stones. Mrs Jordan's favourite role at Richmond was Letitia Hardy in *The Belle's*

Dorothea Jordan, actress and mistress of the Duke of Clarence, later William IV.

Stratagem, a romantic comedy of manners. Her appearances drew packed houses and, it was said, her song 'Where Are You Going To, My Pretty Maid?' was always 'rapturously encored'. On one occasion, on the Duke of Clarence's birthday, it was announced that she could not fill her part because she had to attend a dinner at which the Prince of Orange was guest of honour. The Duke of Clarence also lived for a time at Clarence Lodge in Kew Foot Road and across the river at Bushy House in Bushy Park. He and Dorothea had at least ten children together.

According to the *Oxford Dictionary of National Biography*, when the Duke married Princess Adelaide of Saxe Meiningen, Mrs Jordan was given an annual allowance of £4,400 (close to £800,000 today) by him and custody of their daughters, while he retained custody of their sons. In return she had to promise to give up the stage. However, when she broke the agreement and returned to the theatre to help her son-in-law, who had become seriously in debt, the duke cancelled her stipend and took their daughters into his own care. Later Mrs Jordan's daughter and son-in-law defrauded her by defaulting on large loans they had taken out in her name. She died alone and in poverty. The Duke became William IV in 1830.

DID YOU KNOW?
Vincent van Gogh was a keen Methodist and, while living in Isleworth in 1876, he preached and ran Sunday schools at a number of churches including the Wesleyan Methodist Church in Petersham. On one occasion he walked there from Turnham Green, where he had taught Sunday school, and wrote to his brother Theo: 'It grew dark early and I wasn't sure of the way … But, old boy, there was a beautiful little wooden church with a kindly light at the end of that dark road.'

DID YOU KNOW?
James Thomson, author of *Rule Britannia*, lived in Kew Foot Road, Richmond, and is buried in St Mary Magdalene, with a memorial on the west wall of the south aisle. The song forms part of the masque *Alfred*, about Alfred the Great, with music by Thomas Arne and a libretto by Thomson and David Mallet. It was first performed at Cliveden, country home of Frederick, Prince of Wales. While the masque has been forgotten, *Rule Britannia* has remained one of the most popular patriotic songs.

5. Mortlake Tapestry Works

Suthrey House, No. 119 Mortlake High Street, is a building with a remarkable history. It is the only surviving part of the Mortlake Tapestry Works, once among the very greatest centres of artistic endeavour in England.

In the seventeenth century, tapestry was considered the very highest of art forms, and the finest artists including Van Dyke and Raphael created designs for them. Yet, until 1619, England had no tapestry industry, and these sumptuous works were all imported from Brussels and Paris. James I and his son Charles, Prince of Wales, set out to rival the French King Henry IV, under whose patronage tapestry weaving had flourished in France since 1607.

A site was chosen on the riverside at Mortlake, on the estate of John Dee, who had been an advisor to Elizabeth I, opposite St Mary's Church. Tapestry Court now occupies part of the area used.

The only surviving part of the Mortlake Tapestry Works, in Mortlake High Street.

At one time a pub occupied part of the old tapestry works site.

FRANCESCO CLEYN.

Mortlake's head designer Francis Cleyn. (Yale Centre for British Art)

Mortlake was chosen for several reasons. It was well-placed for communication with the royal palaces along the river, halfway between Hampton Court and Whitehall. The river also facilitated the transport of raw materials and finished work, and the humidity aided the manufacturing process. The main works was a substantial, three-storey building with eighteen looms on the top floor, where light was best.

Also, Mortlake was a familiar location. The Archbishops of Canterbury had been lords of Mortlake manor for centuries and had a manor house just upriver, on the eastern side of Ship Lane where the Stag Brewery was later built. Several monarchs were familiar with the house, and Thomas Cromwell had lived there when he became lord of the manor in 1536.

James I tasked the courtier, entrepreneur and MP Sir Francis Crane (c. 1579–1636), with establishing and administering the works, granting him a monopoly on the production and sale of tapestries for twenty-one years, excusing him from paying customs duties and tax, and giving him the income from four baronetcies.

Nevertheless, the task Crane had been set was a daunting one. There was no pool of skilled labour he could draw upon in England, and he had to look oversees. In great secrecy, around fifty highly-skilled Flemish weavers were recruited and brought from Belgium and Holland. Apprentices were recruited from London orphanages and trained for seven years.

In the early years, Mortlake concentrated on copying tapestries collected by Henry VIII and adding decorative borders to them but, in 1623, Prince Charles bought a series of existing cartoons – drawings which formed the patterns for tapestries – of the Acts of the Apostles which had been made in the workshop of Raphael, the Italian Renaissance painter and architect.

The Destruction of the Children of Niobe from a set of 'The Horses' by Francis Cleyn. (Metropolitan Museum of Art)

Mortlake
tapestries were
renowned
for their
finely crafted
borders.
(Metropolitan
Museum
of Art)

DID YOU KNOW?
There was a second Mortlake house with Thomas Cromwell associations. Old
Cromwell House stood on the site of the former Stag Brewery, facing Williams
Lane. Barnes and Mortlake History Society say the house was lived in by Cromwell's
sister Katherine and her brewer husband, Morgan Williams. There were also
connections with Oliver Cromwell, in that two captains in his army lived there and
he is said to have hidden here when his life was in danger. It was demolished in
1857. The original gateway to Old Cromwell House still stands, but was moved to a
new location in Williams Lane.

The gateway from Cromwell House.

Mortlake entered its golden age in 1626 when Prince Charles poached the hugely accomplished artist Francis Cleyn – whose name was also spelled Clein or Klein – from the king of Denmark as chief designer, building him a family home opposite the works and beside the church. Under Cleyn's direction, Mortlake tapestries were renowned for the quality of their wool, silk and gold-thread yarns, their fine detail, striking colours and borders. As the *Oxford Dictionary of National Biography* notes,

> Cleyn's work appears to have been unrivalled, have always been greatly admired, and some modern authorities have had no hesitation in ascribing them to the hand of Anthony Van Dyck or some more famous painter, ignoring the fact that Cleyn was spoken of at the time as a second Titian, and as 'il famosissimo pittore, miracolo del secolo' [the most famous artist, miracle of the century]. Cleyn was also widely employed by the nobility to decorate their mansions.

Among those mansions was Ham House, where he painted the ceiling of the Green Closet, used to house a collection of miniatures, in the style of Raphael. By 1636 there were 140 Flemish weavers at work. They lived in Mortlake with their families, and the Archbishop of Canterbury allowed Flemish priests to conduct services for them in St Mary's, over the road from the works.

Cartoons were commissioned from the Flemish artist Peter Paul Rubens and Anthony Van Dyck. Generally, tapestries told a story over several panels, and the cartoons for them could be used many times. It is a testament to the brilliance of the work produced at

Francis Cleyn's work can be seen at Richmond's Ham House. (Duncan Harris under Creative Commons 2.0)

Services in Dutch were held for Flemish weavers at St Mary's.

Mortlake that, today, a third of the tapestries in the Royal Collection were woven here, and hang at St James's Palace, Kensington Palace, Windsor Castle and Holyrood Palace, the monarch's official residence in Scotland.

Charles I, who became king in 1625, maintained his great interest in Mortlake, and visited the works in 1629. In 1636, a year after Sir Francis Crane had died and the works had passed to his brother Richard, the king bought the building, renamed it The King's Works, and put Cleyn's salary up from £100 to £250. Cleyn's sons Francis and John worked with him.

However, when Charles was deposed in 1649 after the end of the Second English Civil War, and executed, Mortlake's fortunes plummeted. Under Cromwell's Commonwealth, in which England, Wales, and later Ireland and Scotland were governed as a republic until 1660, tapestries were not commissioned, and Cleyn was employed designing and etching illustrations for books.

Without the royal commissions that had sustained the works, many weavers moved to London. Cleyn moved to Henrietta Street in Covent Garden in 1650, where he was close to John Ogilby, for whom he created designs for lavishly illustrated editions of *Aesop's Fables* and works by Virgil. He died and was buried in St Paul's, Covent Garden, in 1658.

After the Restoration of the Monarchy, Charles II added further Mortlake creations to his father's collection of tapestries, but the glory days were over, and the works closed in 1703.

DID YOU KNOW?
The small brick building beside Mortlake railway station, now part of the Classic Chrome car showroom, is reputed to have been built as a waiting room for Queen Victoria, Prince Albert and other members of the royal family while on journeys to and from the grace-and-favour residence of White Lodge in Richmond Park.

DID YOU KNOW?
Traditional Thames rowing boats are still made beside the Thames at Richmond Bridge, using techniques handed down through generations of craftsmen. The royal barge *Gloriana*, lead ship in the 2012 Thames Diamond Jubilee Pageant, was built by a team led by Mark Edwards of Richmond Bridge Boathouses.

6. Three Remarkable Explorers

Three men who vastly expanded our knowledge of the world are buried in the borough: Sir Richard Burton at Mortlake, and George Vancouver and Henry Lidgbird Ball at Petersham. While Vancouver is hugely famous in Canada, and Ball in Australia, they are little-known figures in Britain.

Sir Richard Burton

It would be hard to imagine a man who, from the evidence of his life and beliefs, was less likely to end up buried in the Catholic cemetery at St Mary Magdalene, Mortlake. As Sir Richard Burton's biographer Fawn Brodie writes in *The Devil Drives,*

The unique tomb of Sir Richard and Isabel Burton.

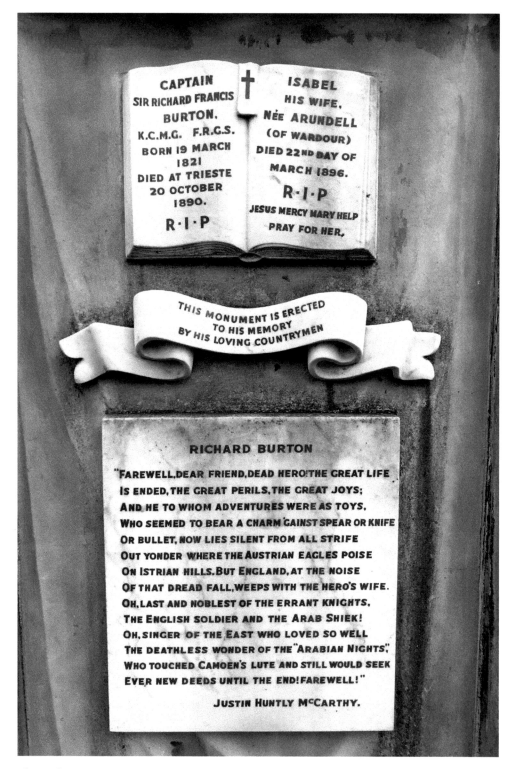

CAPTAIN
SIR RICHARD FRANCIS
BURTON,
K.C.M.G. F.R.G.S.
BORN 19 MARCH
1821
DIED AT TRIESTE
20 OCTOBER
1890.

R·I·P

ISABEL
HIS WIFE,
NÉE ARUNDELL
(OF WARDOUR)
DIED 22ND DAY OF
MARCH 1896.

R·I·P

JESUS MERCY MARY HELP
PRAY FOR HER,

THIS MONUMENT IS ERECTED
TO HIS MEMORY
BY HIS LOVING COUNTRYMEN

RICHARD BURTON

"FAREWELL, DEAR FRIEND, DEAD HERO! THE GREAT LIFE
IS ENDED, THE GREAT PERILS, THE GREAT JOYS;
AND HE TO WHOM ADVENTURES WERE AS TOYS,
WHO SEEMED TO BEAR A CHARM 'GAINST SPEAR OR KNIFE
OR BULLET, NOW LIES SILENT FROM ALL STRIFE
OUT YONDER WHERE THE AUSTRIAN EAGLES POISE
ON ISTRIAN HILLS. BUT ENGLAND, AT THE NOISE
OF THAT DREAD FALL, WEEPS WITH THE HERO'S WIFE.
OH, LAST AND NOBLEST OF THE ERRANT KNIGHTS,
THE ENGLISH SOLDIER AND THE ARAB SHIEK!
OH, SINGER OF THE EAST WHO LOVED SO WELL
THE DEATHLESS WONDER OF THE "ARABIAN NIGHTS",
WHO TOUCHED CAMOEN'S LUTE AND STILL WOULD SEEK
EVER NEW DEEDS UNTIL THE END! FAREWELL!"

JUSTIN HUNTLY McCARTHY.

The tomb inscription.

The combination of Christian and Islamic symbols on the tomb.

Burton scoffed at all forms of religious superstition ... he dwelt fascinated upon all things accounted devilish in his own time. Once he even contemplated writing a biography of Satan.

By some accounts, he even looked like the Devil:

Burton's own visage seems to have conjured up thoughts of Satan; Swinburn said that he had the jaw of a devil and the brow of a god; and the Earl of Dunraven wrote that Burton 'prided himself on looking like Satan – as, indeed, he did'.

Burton's mausoleum – in the shape of a Bedouin tent carved from Forest of Dean stone and Carrara marble – is as out of place in an English churchyard as its occupant. It is only through the determination of his wife, Isabel, that Sir Richard is buried in Mortlake, and the story of how he got here – after a thirty-year battle of wills with her – is as intriguing as anything Burton did during his life.

Sir Richard Burton (1821–90) was a hugely controversial figure with a mania for discovery who challenged and shocked the Victorian establishment. Yet he was a true Renaissance man, and his achievements are remarkable. Brodie says of him,

He was soldier, explorer, ethnologist, archaeologist, poet, translator, and one of the two or three greatest linguists of his time ... [who] sought out the few remaining mysteries ... He penetrated the sacred cities of Mecca and Medina [and performed the Haj disguised as a Muslim pilgrim] at great risk and wrote detailed descriptions. He was the first European to explore the forbidden Muslim city of Harar in Somaliland, which promised death to any infidel. He sought the source of the White Nile, something that had fascinated and defeated Alexander, Caesar and Napoleon.

Equally controversially, 'he took it upon himself to bring to the West the sexual wisdom of the East', producing unexpurgated translations of the *Kama Sutra*, *The Perfumed Garden*, and *One Thousand and One Nights*.

Prior to his interment in Mortlake, Sir Richard's only previous connection with the borough of Richmond was as a schoolboy. In 1829, at the age of eight, he and his brother Edward were enrolled at an obscure institution designed to prepare boys for Eton and Oxford on Richmond Green, run by Revd Charles Delafosse.

The school occupied a mansion at the corner of Little Green and Duke Street and, while the boys were enrolled there, the Burton family rented No. 2 Maids of Honour Row, just across the Green. Burton hated the school, later calling it 'a nightmare', likening it to something from the pen of Charles Dickens, and saying it made him 'fierce, surly and desperate'. He went on:

Instead of learning anything at this school, my brother and I lost much of what we knew ... and the principal acquisitions were, a certain facility of using our fists, and a general development of ruffianism.

A year after the Burton brothers' arrival, the school was hit by a severe measles epidemic, in which several boys died. The Burtons were sent home temporarily, but never returned, the family leaving for France, where they had lived previously.

Burton's rebelliousness and irreverence surfaced again when he was at Trinity College, Oxford, and led to his expulsion. What saved him was his remarkable gift for languages. He could learn a new one in two months and, over his lifetime, mastered around thirty-five, learning and discarding them in turn. Arabic was not taught at Oxford, so Burton taught himself, and then followed a career as a Foreign Office diplomat. As an explorer he ranked alongside David Livingstone and Henry Stanley but, says Brodie,

> Burton's real passion was not for geographical discovery but for the hidden truth in man, for the unknowable, and inevitably the unthinkable. What his Victorian compatriots called unclean, bestial, or satanic he regarded with almost clinical detachment.

Yet he married Isabel Arundell, a member of the Catholic aristocracy, in what was 'a love marriage in the most absolute sense of the word'. Isabel laid out her reasons for marrying Richard in her journals, writing, 'my ideal [is] of being a companion and wife, a life of travel adventure and danger, seeing and learning, with love to glorify it; that is what I seek'.

Above left: Sir Richard Burton. (Wellcome Collection)

Above right: Burton's controversial translation of *One Thousand and One Nights*.

She only told her parents after her secret wedding, at the Royal Bavarian Chapel – now known as Our Lady of the Assumption and St Gregory – in Warwick Street, Westminster, apologising for 'flying in the face of God'. She hoped, says Brodie, to make Burton 'powerful, respectable and catholic'. Yet her determination to bring him into her church was matched by Burton's to resist.

Although he would teasingly raise her hopes by, for example, wearing a medal of the Virgin Mary round his neck, or crying during midnight Mass, he continued to show his contempt for the Catholic Church in his writings. Indeed, says Brodie, Richard 'was as intent on winning her away from the church as she was to salvage his soul'.

Burton was jealous of Isabel going to confession and, determined to discover his wife's innermost thoughts, turned to hypnosis. Isabel wrote, 'Once mesmerised, he had only to say, "Talk", and I used to tell him everything.'

As Burton aged, his health weakened. He suffered a series of serious heart attacks and Isabel feared increasingly that he would die without being baptised a Catholic – before, as she put it, 'I could save Richard's soul'. She did, however, manage to persuade him to buy a plot in the Catholic cemetery at Mortlake, where several members of her family were buried. While they were on holiday in Cannes, in 1887, Richard suffered a further severe heart attack. Isabel wrote, 'I got some water, and knelt down and saying some prayers, I baptised him.'

Lady Isabel Burton. (Inductiveload via Creative Commons 2.0)

Isabel bought No. 2 Worple Road to be close to Richard's resting place.

However, she knew that would not be enough for the church so when, in Trieste in 1890, he suffered his final, fatal heart attack, she begged the doctor to keep him alive, by applying an electric battery to his heart, for the two hours it took for a priest to arrive. Initially, the priest told her he could not administer extreme unction – as the application of holy chrism oil was then termed – because Burton had not declared himself a Catholic, and was now dead. When Isabel said she had evidence Richard was secretly a convert, and insisted he was still alive, the priest relented.

She wanted him buried in Westminster Abbey, along with other great explorers, but the church authorities turned her down, aware of his public condemnation of organised religion. Isabel decided, instead, to create a monument for Richard at Mortlake. Remembering that he had once said to her 'I should like us both to lie in a tent, side by side', she designed an exotic tomb, 18 feet high and 12 feet square. His body was placed in the church's crypt until the tomb was finished, and the funeral was held on 15 June 1891.

Isabel visited every Sunday and held seances in an attempt to contact Richard. In order to be close to him at all times she bought a little terraced house opposite the churchyard at No. 2 Worple Road, which she called 'Our Cottage'. When she died, in 1896, Isabel's coffin was placed alongside Richard's. She also commissioned a memorial stained-glass window for the church, in which Richard is depicted as a medieval knight. His personal effects, and paintings, photographs and objects relating to him are held in the Burton Collection at Orleans House Gallery, Twickenham.

DID YOU KNOW?
Until 1777, when Richmond Bridge was built, a ferry operated at this point. The right to run it was given to William Windham by George II, as a curious form of 'thank you'. Windham's wife had been the king's mistress, and Windham had tutored George's son, Prince William, Duke of Cumberland.

George Vancouver

George Vancouver is another man of enormous achievement who is buried here by pure chance. In a great voyage of exploration lasting from 1791–95, Vancouver sailed his ship HMS *Discovery* around Africa's Cape of Good Hope and, as John Cloake recorded in *Richmond's Links with North America*,

[He] surveyed the south-west coast of Australia and the New Zealand coastline, filling in gaps which Cook had left undiscovered, he made for Tahiti the Hawaiian Islands and then for the western cost of North America. For two years he explored and mapped the coast north of San Francisco right up to Alaska, circumnavigating the island which bears his name, and finally returned to England via Cape Horn and St Helena.

Hence the city and island of Vancouver in British Columbia are named after him, as is Vancouver in Washington state USA, Mount Vancouver on the Canadian-American border of Yukon and Alaska, and New Zealand's sixth highest mountain.

Yet, just three years after these remarkable achievements, Vancouver – whose father was Dutch and whose surname derives from van Coevorden, meaning originating

CAPTAIN GEORGE VANCOUVER

Died in the Year 1798,

Aged 40.

RESTORED BY
THE NATIVE SONS OF
BRITISH COLUMBIA,
POST NO. 2 (CANADA)
MAINTAINED BY THE LATE
MAJOR J.S. MATTHEWS
AND THE CITY OF VANCOUVER,
B.C. (CANADA)

George Vancouver's grave at St Peter's, Petersham.

Vancouver spent his last years at Glen Cottage, River Lane.

from the Netherlands city of Coevorden – was wandering aimlessly in Britain when he happened to stay at the then hugely fashionable Star and Garter Hotel on Richmond Hill.

Vancouver (1757–98) was already a sick man, and was looking for a place to write his memoirs. When he awoke the morning after his arrival and looked out of his hotel window at the view from Richmond Hill, he realised he had found it. He wrote, 'In all my travels I have never clept eyes on a more beautiful spot than this! Here would I live and here would I die.'

He leased Glen Cottage, in River Lane, Petersham. Life there was uneventful until, one day, a man turned up at his door and challenged him to a duel. The man was Thomas Pitt, Lord Camelford, who as a midshipman on the *Discovery* had been flogged and discharged by Vancouver for disobeying orders. Vancouver refused to fight but Camelford pursued him, and a series of confrontations occurred. Finally, Camelford assaulted Vancouver in Conduit Street, London W1, an event which was caricatured by James Gillray in a drawing entitled 'The caneing in Conduit Street. Dedicated to the flag officers of the British Navy'. Gillray's interest in the episode reflected the growing opposition to harsh naval discipline. Camelford was bound over to keep the peace in the sum of £10,000.

Vancouver was only forty when he died at his home on 10 May 1798. He is buried at St Peter's in Petersham. Recognition of Vancouver's greatness has only come slowly in Richmond. In 1841 the Hudson Bay Company erected a memorial plaque in the church. In 1936, on the fiftieth anniversary of the establishment of the city of Vancouver, a special ceremony was held at the churchyard, and a painting of the grave presented to the city.

A commemorative coin and stamp honouring George Vancouver.

Vancouver's Portland stone grave was restored in the 1960s, and Grade II listed in recognition of its historical importance. A commemorative service is held annually on the Sunday closest to Vancouver's death.

DID YOU KNOW?
John Aubrey, in his 1719 publication *The Natural History and Antiquities of the County of Surrey*, says that while Petersham was under the monks of Chertsey Abbey, pre-Reformation it was a place of sanctuary, in which no one could be arrested. Nor could anyone already under arrest be brought through the village.

Henry Lidgbird Ball

Henry Lidgbird Ball is famed Down Under as the commander of HMS *Supply*, one of the eleven ships of the First Fleet, which set sail from Portsmouth on 13 May 1787 and founded the first European settlement in Australia. Like George Vancouver, Ball is buried at St Peter's, Petersham.

Henry Lidgbird Ball's grave is hidden behind others.

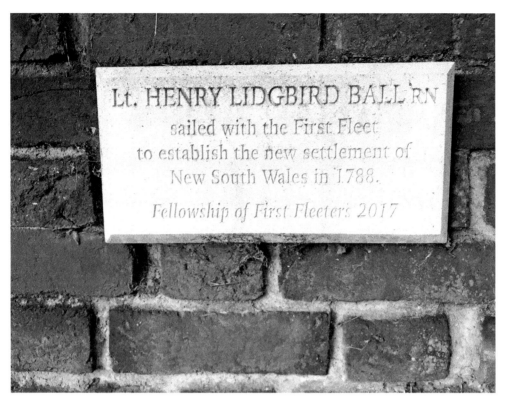

A plaque honouring Henry Lidgbird Ball, placed here in 2017.

The First Fleet brought between 1,000 and 1,500 convicts, seamen and free settlers (accounts of the actual total differ) to Australia. Ball's ship took 250 days to make the voyage to New South Wales, arriving at Port Jackson, on Sydney Harbour, on 18 January 1788.

Ball (1756–1818) explored extensively around Port Jackson. On one expedition he took part in the capture of an Aborigine, Arabanoo, at Manly Cove. The Governor, Arthur Phillip, claimed the forcible abduction was necessary in order to end the 'state of petty warfare and endless uncertainty' that existed between the native Eora people and settlers. He said,

> It was absolutely necessary that we should attain their language, or teach them ours that the means of redress might be pointed out to them, if they are injured, and to reconcile them by showing the many advantages they would enjoy by mixing with us.

In fact, Arabanoo learned little English and, after six months, died of smallpox.

Ball discovered the twenty-eight islands in the Lord Howe group, between Australia and New Zealand, while en route from Botany Bay to found another penal colony on Norfolk Island. An uninhabited, volcanic island in the Lord Howe chain is named Ball's Pyramid after him, as are Ball's Bay on Norfolk Island and Ball's Point in Sydney Harbour.

He gained notoriety when he married a convict, Sarah Partridge, who had been sentenced to death, commuted to transportation for seven years, for stealing a length of expensive fabric from a shop in London. The stolen goods were valued at £9 (equivalent to £1,300 today). Sarah denied the charge, and the record of the proceedings at the Old Bailey does leave room to doubt the safety of the conviction. She and two other women had left the shop before the theft was discovered, and were followed by a clerk to a house, where the cloth was lying on a table. Sarah was convicted on the grounds that she had been closest to the fabric while in the shop.

In Australia, Sarah lived with Ball on his ship and, in 1789, gave birth to a daughter, Ann Maria. Sarah appears to have died in Australia, but Ann travelled back with her father to England when he was discharged in 1791. Also on his ship was the first kangaroo to be brought to England.

Ball was to marry twice more back home, his second wife dying just a year after their marriage. In 1810 he married his third wife, Anne Johnston, thirty-one years his junior, in Kingston-upon-Thames. He was buried in his wife's family vault at Petersham in 1818. In 2013 a commemorative plaque to Henry Lidgbird Ball was added to the Johnston tomb at a service attended by Australia's High Commissioner to the UK.

DID YOU KNOW?
Petersham used to be connected with Richmond via a causeway because the road under the hill became impassable to pedestrians in winter.

7. Charles Darwin, and the Plot to Destroy Kew Gardens

Above: Kew's Palm House. (David Iliff, license CC BY-SA 3.0)

Right: Charles Darwin. (Wellcome Collection)

Kew director Sir Joseph
Dalton Hooker.
(Wellcome Collection)

Sir Joseph Dalton Hooker was director of the Royal Botanic Gardens at Kew, and Charles Darwin's closest friend. Hooker's support for Darwin's then controversial and divisive theories on evolution was a key factor in a concerted campaign to destroy Hooker's reputation, and have the Royal Botanic Gardens reduced to a mere amusement park.

If the plan had succeeded, the remarkable work Kew has done over many decades on plant discovery, categorisation and conservation would have been nipped in the bud. To look at Hooker's achievements today it is hard to imagine that such a thing could have happened, yet the threat was very real.

Sir Joseph (1817–1911) took over Kew from his father, William Jackson Hooker, in 1865 and ran it for twenty years. He was a towering man of science and the leading botanist of his age. Before taking over at Kew he had explored widely. Hooker gathered around 7,000 species of plants from India, and was the first westerner to explore the remote northern Himalayas, where his curiosity led to his being imprisoned.

He gathered valuable information and samples across the world: from Palestine and Morocco to the United States, Antarctica, and New Zealand. He published seminal works including the seven-volume *Flora of British India*, the *Student's Flora of the British Isles*, the *Genera Plantarum* which covered the vast collections at Kew and completed *The Handbook of the British flora*, which had been begun by George Bentham and would become the standard text for a hundred years.

Hooker was showered with honours. He was president of the Royal Society, was made Knight Grand Commander of the Order of the Star of India and, in 1907 at the age of ninety, was awarded the Order of Merit.

A plan of Kew Gardens in Hooker's time. (Wellcome Collection)

A botanical drawing of the flat peach of China, by Hooker. (Wellcome Collection)

Sir Richard Owen, Hooker and Darwin's deadly rival. (Wellcome Collection)

How then could his position have been challenged? It was because the great reputation he built for himself, and for Kew, provoked the jealousy of the British Museum's superintendent of natural history, Richard Owen. Owen believed Kew should be subordinate to the British Museum, and that Hooker should answer to him. As foreign plant specimens flooded in to the herbarium at Kew, eclipsing the collection Owen was amassing – and the work he was doing – at the museum, he argued that Hooker should not be allowed to develop a scientific institution with a great botanic garden as an independent entity.

A bitter rivalry developed, and became extremely personal. Hooker countered Owen's proposal by arguing, in 1868, that the enormous collection of 30,000 specimens amassed by the naturalist Joseph Banks was being mismanaged at the British Museum, and should be moved to Kew. The idea threatened to undermine Owen's plans to create a Natural History Museum in South Kensington.

Owen took his campaign against Hooker to the top of government. He enlisted the support of Acton Smee Ayrton, an MP who, having been appointed by Prime Minister William Gladstone as First Commissioner of Works in 1869, was responsible for funding Kew, and was Hooker's boss. Ayrton pursued a campaign against Hooker, interfering in the running of Kew by taking on responsibility for staff appointments and seeking to cut its budgets. His aim was to curtail its scientific work and reduce it to a mere pleasure garden. He hoped to get Kew's director to resign, something Hooker seriously considered, writing, 'My life has become utterly detestable and I do long to throw up the directorship. What can be more humiliating than two years of wrangling with such a creature!'

Did you know?
Richmond resident Elihu Yale endowed the American university which bears his name. John Cloake, in *Richmond's Links with North America*, reports that Yale, who moved in 1712 into a mansion on Richmond Green, where Portland Terrace now stands, was considering endowing an Oxford college, but was persuaded to divert his funds to a new college to be established in New Haven, Connecticut. However, the cash hoped for did not materialise. Instead, Yale gave books, a portrait of the king and other items which the university could sell to raise funds.

Hooker and Darwin

Apart from the turf war Owen was fighting against Hooker, there was also the issue of Hooker's support for the theories on evolution and natural selection expounded in Charles Darwin's *On the Origin of Species*, published in 1859.

Relations between Hooker and Darwin had been close for years. They began corresponding in 1843, when Hooker was twenty-six and Darwin thirty-four, and wrote 1,400 letters to each other over forty years. As the Darwin Correspondence Project records,

Darwin's theories were parodied widely.
(Wellcome Collection)

The Herbarium at Kew, into which flooded samples collected by explorers. (Michael Dibb under Creative Commons 2.0)

their communication began when Hooker 'was approached about working on Darwin's collection of plants from the Beagle voyage [to the Galapagos islands]'. They note,

> Just the previous year Darwin had written out his first coherent account of the main elements of his species theory, and within a few months Hooker was admitted into the small and select group of those with whom Darwin felt able to discuss his emerging ideas. In perhaps his most famous letter of all, Darwin wrote to Hooker in January 1844 of his growing conviction that species 'are not ... immutable' – an admission he likened, half-jokingly, to 'confessing a murder'. When Alfred Russel Wallace (1823-1913) sent Darwin a letter in 1858 outlining an almost identical theory to his own, it was Hooker, together with Charles Lyell, who engineered the simultaneous publication of papers by both men, and secured Darwin's claim to the theory of 'modification through descent' by means of the mechanism Darwin called 'natural selection'.

On his India expedition, Hooker looked in the world's highest mountains for evidence to support Darwin's theory. As controller of Kew he 'was perfectly placed to provide Darwin with exotic species, and to help him build vital global networks of well-informed correspondents'.

Hooker was one of the few people Darwin showed drafts of his manuscript to in the years before publication. There was almost a disaster when Hooker's children used some of the manuscript of *On the Origin of Species* to draw on.

Hooker was a member of the X Club, a group of hugely influential scientists, biologists, mathematicians and others united by 'a devotion to science, pure and free, untrammelled by religious dogmas'. They propounded naturalism, the belief that the world operates according to natural, rather than supernatural or spiritual, forces and laws. They supported Darwin's theories, and sought to get them accepted by an establishment that saw in them a grave threat to their creationist faith, and was outraged at the suggestion that men might be descended from apes.

Finally, Darwin and X Club members exposed the plot against Hooker to Gladstone's private secretary. The House of Lords demanded to see the correspondence between Owen and Ayrton, and it was revealed that Ayrton had commissioned from Owen an official report on Kew, which was kept secret from Hooker, who was therefore robbed of any right of reply. The report attacked both Hooker and his father and claimed

Acton Smee Ayrton waged a campaign against Hooker. (Wellcome Collection)

Darwin and others appealed to
Prime Minister William Gladstone to
save Kew Gardens.

Today, features including a treetop
walkway have made Kew a huge
attraction. (Stephen Boisvert under
Creative Commons 2.0)

erroneously, among many other things, that they had mismanaged the care of their trees, and that their systematic approach to botany was nothing more than 'attaching barbarous binomials to foreign weeds'.

When asked why the report had been kept from Hooker, Ayrton said that he 'was too low an official to raise questions of matter with a Minister of the Crown'. Hooker was able to refute all the allegations in the report, and won the support of both parliament and the press. Ayrton was removed from the Board of Works and failed to get re-elected as an MP. The Royal Botanic Gardens was safe, and the value of its work has never since been questioned.

DID YOU KNOW?
Maids of Honour tarts, baked to a traditional Richmond recipe with a puff pastry shell filled with sweetened cheese curds, are said to have been a favourite of Henry VIII. They are sold at the Original Maids of Honour restaurant, established in the early eighteenth century, initially in Hill Street. Robert Newens, an apprentice at the shop, went on to open his own premises in King Street, and then at No. 3 George Street. In 1887 his son Alfred opened the premises on Kew Road from which the tarts have been sold to this day.

Maids of Honour tarts. (Amanda Slater under Creative Commons 2.0)

DID YOU KNOW?
Sir David Attenborough unwittingly solved a notorious Victorian murder mystery when, while excavating the site of a former pub he was turning into a wildlife garden alongside his home in Park Road in 2010, workmen uncovered the skull of Julia Martha Thomas, killed in 1879. The site was within 100 yards of where Mrs Thomas was murdered, chopped up and boiled by her housekeeper, Kate Webster. Various body parts were found in Richmond, but the head remained undiscovered.

8. Richmond's Compassion for the Victims of War

Richmond has been home to two hugely significant organisations dedicated to helping those suffering as a result of war. One, the British Legion Poppy Factory, is still going strong. The other, the Royal Star and Garter Home, moved on in recent years.

DID YOU KNOW?
The Royal Observatory in Old Deer Park played a vital part in the victory over Germany in the Second World War, when it was home to the Meteorological Office. General Eisenhower based his decision to go ahead with the D-Day landings on 5 June 1944 after a twenty-eight-year-old meteorologist based there, Group Captain J. M. Stagg, accurately predicted the bad weather would ease.

The Poppy Factory

Major George Howson knew first-hand the long-term suffering that war could bring to the bravest of men. Howson (1886–1936) had served on the Western Front throughout the First World War, and was awarded the Military Cross for bravery after his unit continued to repair a road while under shellfire, and despite his having received a shrapnel wound, during the Battle of Passchendaele in July 1917.

His wounds were trivial when compared to those of Major Jack Cohen MP, who lost both legs at Ypres. Howson and Cohen lobbied the government to improve the quality of artificial limbs. Howson drew on his practical abilities – before the war he had attended Heriot-Watt Engineering College, Edinburgh, and managed a rubber estate in Borneo – to produce a guide for artificial limbs that would be lighter, more practical, and comfortable.

Howson also recognised that disabled veterans faced depression and financial hardship unless they could find work and, in 1920 when Howson retired from the army, the pair founded the Disabled Society. The goal was to provide work and practical support.

Things began to come together when, after the first Poppy Appeal in 1921 used artificial flowers imported from France, the British Legion commissioned the Disabled Society to make poppies in England for the following year. *The Oxford Dictionary of National Biography* records just how daunting Howson saw the challenge before him. He wrote the following to his parents:

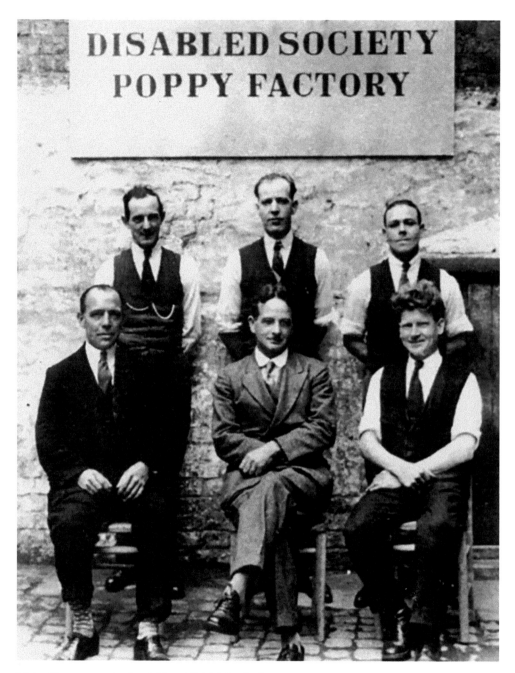

Major Howson, centre front. (Royal British Legion)

It is a large responsibility and will be very difficult. If the experiment is successful it will be the start of an industry to employ 150 disabled men. I do not think it can be a great success but it is worth trying. I consider the attempt ought to be made if only to give the disabled their chance. I have to find a factory tomorrow and interview men.

The Poppy Factory. (Nick Eaglesfield under Creative Commons 2.0)

Howson found premises in a disused collar factory in the Old Kent Road, and quickly acquired knowledge of how the artificial flower trade worked. In an industry which employed girls on minimal wages, Howson was determined to pay full male wages. He also used his 'practical genius for ergonomics' to come up with a design that could be assembled using just one hand. Beginning with five ex-service employees, he rapidly built a staff of forty who made a million poppies in two months. In 1924 they made 27 million.

The following year the Disabled Society merged with the British Legion, and in 1926 Howson found new, larger premises in Richmond, at a former brewery at No. 20 Petersham Road. The site, in a pleasant spot alongside the Thames and close to Richmond Park, was carefully chosen to aid recovery and rehabilitation. He also built homes alongside the factory for veterans employed there and their families, and the complex included a cinema and pub. The men Howson employed had an average incapacity of between 60 and 70 per cent and, despite a policy of taking only the most severely disabled, the waiting list grew and grew.

All this required large sums of money which, thankfully, Howson had. In 1918 he had married Jessie Gibson, daughter of William Gibson, owner of the Foy & Gibson chain of department stores in Australia. When her father died in November 1918, Jessie inherited great wealth, and the couple were able to put the money to good use at Richmond. In 1928 Howson established the Field of Remembrance at Westminster Abbey, which quickly became the site of the central ceremony of respect and homage to the nation's war dead, and the factory began producing remembrance wreaths and crosses in addition to poppies.

Above and below: Working in the factory in 1935, and today. (Royal British Legion, Mike Weston)

Housing for veterans was built alongside the factory.

While showing great concern for the health of others, Howson neglected his own, which had been poor ever since he had contracted malaria and dysentery in Borneo before the war. He was a heavy smoker of strong Turkish cigarettes – which he bought in batches of 10,000 – and by the 1930s was suffering from cancer of the pancreas. When the time came for him to enter a hospice, Howson asked the ambulance to take him first to the Poppy Factory. As *The Times* reported, he was able to sit up in the ambulance and the 365 veterans then making 29 million poppies a year gathered round for a sing-song. As the ambulance drove off he struck up the singing of 'Are We Downhearted?.'

Today, while around thirty disabled veterans work at the factory – plus the same number of home-workers – and produce 11 million poppies plus over a million wreaths and other remembrance symbols, many hundreds are helped in other ways. Since 2010 the Poppy Factory has run a Getting You Back to Work service, which has helped over a thousand veterans find jobs in their own communities. A team of regional employment consultants provide advice, coaching, and identify openings with local employers.

The Poppy Factory stands today as a monument to George Howson's enterprise, humanity, philanthropy and sheer practical ability.

DID YOU KNOW?
In the late 1940s Wick House, next door to the similarly named The Wick on Richmond Hill, became a home for twenty nurses at the Royal Star and Garter Home.

Royal Star and Garter Home

Like the Poppy Factory, the Royal Star and Garter Home on Richmond Hill catered for the most profound casualties of war. As Simon Fowler writes in *The Valhalla of British Heroism: the early years of the Star and Garter Home*,

> At the outbreak of the Great War there was very little provision for permanently disabled soldiers and sailors. On the whole, they were expected to be cared for by their families: unlucky men would probably end up in the workhouse. However, as casualties mounted in 1914 and 1915 it became clear that there was nowhere where men permanently disabled by their service in the armed forces could see out their days. A network of hospitals and convalescent homes looked after wounded men, but this care ceased when soldiers and sailors were discharged from the services.

Among those concerned at their plight was Queen Mary, wife of George V, who asked that a 'permanent haven' might be set up for them. The members of the Auctioneers and Estate Agents Institute responded, and within a few weeks raised £21,000 (around £1.8 million today, according to the Bank of England's Inflation Calculator) to buy the former Star and Garter Hotel on Richmond Hill. The premises were presented to the queen, who handed them on to the British Red Cross Society.

However, there were problems. The hotel was nowhere as easy to convert into a hospital as had been anticipated. Only an annex housing the former hotel's banqueting hall and ballroom could be used initially, and there was room for only sixty-four patients, far fewer than had been anticipated. Sir Frederick Treves, chairman of the home's board of governors and surgeon to the king, who had hoped that this would be a 'Hampton Court Palace for disabled soldiers', said,

The former Star and Garter home from the river.

The Star and Garter Hotel, which once occupied the site.

> I found the old building quite impossible to adapt to the requirements of a modern hospital for the reasons that the basement was dank, very badly ventilated and in other ways unsuitable. One could hardly have asked the domestic personnel to take up their duties in the basement.

In July 1915, the British Women's Hospital Committee set about raising the £50,000 (£4.3 million today) needed to bring the buildings up to standard. In fact, they managed to raise £223,948 (roughly £20 million today), and an annex was built that doubled capacity, but the full demolition and rebuilding that was needed would have to wait until after the war.

Despite the problems, remarkable work was done in those early years at the Star and Garter. The first patients were admitted on 14 January 1916 and by June the home was full. Most patients were men who had been shot in the spine or brain, were often paralysed below the waist, and had been discharged from the services as incurable.

However, the doctors and nursing staff believed no case was hopeless. A staff of ten therapists administered long-term massage, passive exercise and electrotherapy. Occupations such as leatherwork, basketry and other handicrafts were used to aid recovery. By the end of the first year, while twenty patients had died, eighteen had been discharged as 'improved' and five 'immensely improved', meaning they were able to walk out. One, Private Harry Mingary, was discharged in September 1916 to marry Nina Bredman, a masseuse who had aided his recovery.

The Star and Garter Hotel from the terrace.

The Star and Garter after fire destroyed much of the hotel.

Anticipating such success, the *Ladies' Pictorial* wrote the following in December 1915:

> Richmond will indeed be proud to have such heroes in her midst, and to share with them the exceptional natural beauties and many interests with which she is so lavishly endowed. When in future visitors come from afar to see Richmond and its world renown view, surely the chief point of interest will be the Star and Garter and its inmates who fought in the Great War.

Work on the new 180-bed home began in 1919, when the existing buildings were demolished, and residents were transferred to a seaside home at Sandgate, Kent, pending completion in 1924. The new Star and Garter Home for Disabled Sailors, Soldiers and Airmen was based on a plan produced by Sir Giles Gilbert Scott – architect of Battersea Power Station and Liverpool's Anglican Cathedral, and designer of the red telephone box – and formally reopened by George V and Queen Mary on 10 July. It only got its Royal prefix in 1979.

During the Second World War the neurologist Dr Ludwig Guttman, a Jewish refugee from Nazi Germany, established a special paraplegic ward at the Star and Garter. Guttman was an early champion of sport as a vital therapy that built strength and self-respect. In 1943 Guttman would go on to found the spinal unit at Stoke Mandeville Hospital. Five years later he established the Grand Festival of Paraplegic Sport, a precursor to the

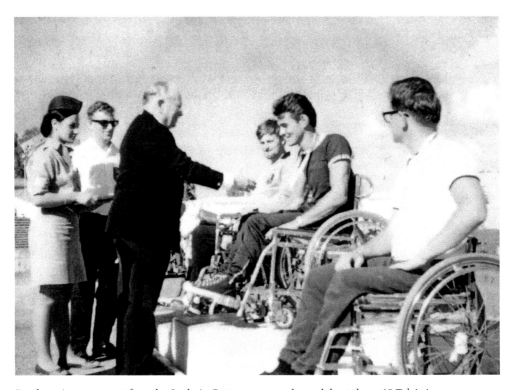

Paralympic movement founder Ludwig Guttmann awards medals at the 1968 Tel Aviv games.

Paralympic Games, in which residents of the Star and Garter competed against Stoke Mandeville for the Challenge Shield.

In the 1950s, the home's workshops were expanded to include watch and clock manufacture and repair, toy production and sock and rug making.

In 2011 the trust which ran the Star and Garter decided to sell the building, which failed to meet modern standards. Residents were transferred to a new purpose-built home in Upper Brighton Road, Surbiton. The trust also runs homes at Solihull, West Midlands, and High Wycombe, Buckinghamshire. In 2013 the Richmond building was sold, for £50 million, to London Square, a housing developer, for conversion into luxury flats.

DID YOU KNOW?
In 1940 1,000 bombed-out East-enders fled to Richmond, but did not receive a warm welcome from some residents reluctant to take Cockney strangers into their homes. Simon Fowler in *Richmond at War 1939-40* says some evacuees preferred to sleep in public shelters, and a number were so homesick they returned downriver to face the Blitz.

Bibliography

Anon., *Darwin Correspondence Project* www.darwinproject.ac.uk/joseph-dalton-hooker

Anon., *Dictionary of National Biography* (Oxford: Oxford University Press, 2004)

Aubrey, John, *The Natural History and Antiquities of the County of Surrey* (London: E Curll, 1719)

Barnes and Mortlake History Society www.barnes-history.org.uk/BandMmap/Cromwell.html

Blake, Mark, *Pigs Might Fly: The Inside Story of Pink Floyd* (London: Aurum Press, 2013)

Brodie, Fawn, *The Devil Drives: A Life of Sir Richard Burton* (London: Eland, 2002)

Cloake, John, *King's Observatory Historical Report* www.kingsobervatory.co.uk

Cloake, John, *Richmond Palace: Its History and Its Plan* (Richmond: Richmond Historical Society, 2001)

Cloake, John, *Richmond's Links with North America* (Richmond: Richmond Local History Society, 1989)

Cundall, H. M., *Bygone Richmond* (London: John Lane, The Bodley Head, 1925)

Faucit, Martin, Helena *On Some of Shakespeare's Female Characters* (London: William Blackwood, 1885)

Fowler, Simon, *Richmond at War 1939-45* (Richmond: Richmond Local History Society, 2015)

Fowler, Simon, *The Valhalla of British Heroism: The Early Years of the Star and Garter Home* (Richmond: Richmond History Society, 1999)

Fullagar, Peter, *Virginia Woolf in Richmond* (Twickenham: Aurora Metro, 2018)

Loewenstein, Rupert, Prince, *A Prince Among Stones* (London: Bloomsbury, 2013)

Pollard, Mary, *Early Performances at Richmond Theatre* (Richmond: Richmond Local History Society, 2019)

Robinson, Derek, *The Richmond Vicars* (Richmond: Richmond Museum, 2019)

Summers, A. Leonard, *The Homes of George Eliot* (London: Folk Press, 1926)

Wilkerson, Mark, *Who Are You: The Life of Pete Townshend* (London: Omnibus Press, 2009)

Wood, Ronnie, *Ronnie* (London: St Martin's Press, 2007)

Woolf, Leonard, *Beginning Again* (New York: Houghton Mifflin, 1989)

Woolf, Virginia, *Diary* (London: Mariner Books, 1979)

Acknowledgements

The author and publishers would like to thank the following people/organisations for permission to use copyright material in this book: the Wellcome Collection for images from its archive plus the many photographers who have made their work available under Creative Commons. I would also like to thank Richmond Council for its invaluable local history notes, the staff of Richmond Local Studies Library, Richmond Local History Society, the Friends of Richmond Green, Barnes and Mortlake History Society, and the Kew Bookshop at No. 1–2 Station Approach, TW9 3QB.

Every attempt has been made to seek permission for copyright material used in this book. However, if we have inadvertently used copyright material without permission/ acknowledgement we apologise and will make the necessary correction at the first opportunity.